Traders' Tales

Traders' Tales

A Chronicle of Wall Street Myths, Legends, and Outright Lies

Ron Insana

John Wiley & Sons, Inc.
New York   Chichester   Brisbane   Toronto   Singapore

Copyright © 1996 by Ron Insana.
Published by John Wiley & Sons, Inc.

All rights reserved. Published simultaneously in Canada.

Library of Congress Cataloging-in-Publication Data:

Insana, Ron.
    Traders' tales: a chronicle of Wall Street myths, legends and outright lies/Ron Insana.
        p.   cm.
    ISBN 0-471-12999-2 (cloth: alk. paper)
    1. Floor traders (Finance—United States.   2. Stockbrokers—United States.   3. Wall Street.   I. Title
    HG4928.5.I53   1996
    332.64'273—dc20   96-3501

Printed in the United States of America

10 9 8 7 6 5 4 3 2 1

To Mom and Dad,
I love you

To Melinda,
my beautiful bride

Preface

In the early 1600s, a small Dutch flotilla landed on the shores of this brave new world. It was manned by a hearty lot of sailors and merchants—traders for the Dutch East India Company. These were brave men who seized opportunities, took risks, and reaped great rewards from the fruits of their labor. In what is now lower Manhattan, this enterprising band of sailing Dutchmen established a thriving colony they called New Amsterdam. It grew into a bustling place of commerce, a thriving port of call for early explorers of the New World.

Being Dutchmen, they had achieved a certain sophistication in financial affairs that was legendary in the Old World. They were explorers, entrepreneurs, speculators, and, of course, great traders. In 1626, led by Peter Minuet, these high-flying Dutchmen fleeced the locals out of the most valuable piece of real estate in history. For twenty-four bucks in beads and trinkets, the Dutch settlers gained control of Manhattan Island, a piece of property that's worth hundreds of billions of dollars today.

Then a rich culture began to grow along the narrow, drafty corridor we now call Wall Street. From its Dutch origins to its British days to its reign as the financial capital of the world, Wall Street has been home to an undeniably colorful and unique populace. It is populated by those who capitalize on chaos, revel in risk, and profit handsomely from the perils of the day. It is a place where fortunes are made and lost, where legends rise and fall—and tales are told to all who will listen.

Preface

Traders' Tales is a collection of stories that captures the true flavor of Wall Street. These tales have been collected from some of the best-known names in the business as well as some people you've probably never heard of. But each story illustrates the atmosphere of the Street. From the humorous escapades of the day traders to some noble lessons from famous investors, *Traders' Tales* is a collection of reminiscences that characterizes our fast-fading Wall Street culture.

For most of its history, Wall Street has been a wild and woolly place. The behavior of its inhabitants reflects the emotional extremes that run rampant through the money capital of the world. The pressure, anxiety, fear, and also greed, produce some unexpected side-effects—from sophomoric behavior in some cases to (economically) heroic acts in others. Life on Wall Street is as charming in its own way as life once was on Main Street, USA.

But the culture on the Street is changing quickly. Where a fraternal order once existed, there is now a more buttoned-down approach to business. Where a man's word once sealed the deal, now computers handle anonymous megatransactions. *Traders' Tales* is an effort to capture the culture of Wall Street as it will always be remembered, not as it may soon be.

Acknowledgments

Whether it's for their thoughts, time, patience, or encouragement, a debt is always owed to many people for a compilation such as this one. First and foremost I must thank my parents, Arthur and Adelia Insana, for their love and for the sacrifices they made so I could gain countless opportunities in life, including the opportunity to write this book. My brother, Art, is also to be thanked for his early and important influence on my life, for his constant inspiration, and for his tireless efforts in helping to edit the manu-

Preface

script. My sister, Lisa, listened to some of my most boring stories, but always patiently cheered me on to complete my work. And, of course, most important in my life is my wife, Melinda, who, while toiling away in the oblivion of the night shift at CNBC, was my source of comfort and encouragement while I hammered away at this "second job."

I must also thank my good friend, mentor, and spiritual guide through life, Douglas Crichton, who has shared much time and much knowledge over the years and who has helped me to formulate much of my current thinking on markets and economics. The late Ed Hart and still-vibrant John Bollinger offered much in that regard as well.

A compilation like *Traders' Tales* is utterly dependent on the traders, investors, analysts, and other practitioners of the financial trade who have graciously shared their stories, remembrances, and personal anecdotes with me. My thanks to all who were so giving of their time.

Several of my friends from the financial world gave freely of their time as well though their tales did not appear in the final manuscript. Still, I would like to thank the following people for their insights and their inspiration: Al Frank, Mario Gabelli, Elaine Garzarelli, Richard Grasso, John Kenneth Galbraith, Henry Kaufman, and Marla Ramirez.

The illustrations in the book were provided by Douglas Pike whose "Doubtful Accounts" cartoons led me to find a new friend in the world of business information. Humor is his stock in trade, while stocks and bonds are mine. I'm sure we'll find mutually profitable ventures again.

Three financial professionals are largely responsible for my first effort in the publishing arena since they, unbeknownst to me, told Myles Thompson of John Wiley & Sons to call me simply because I wanted to write a book. Tom DeMark, Courtney Smith, and Jim Yates, to you three I am forever grateful.

Preface

I am also deeply indebted to Myles who took a chance on an untested author and willingly and quite generously opened an entirely new vista in my life. Myles's stewardship over the project was masterful, and I hope to benefit from his publishing skills again. Jacque Urinyi, who supervised the editing process, was remarkably patient with me and my insecurities as she whittled away at my frequent redundancies. Both she and Myles, quite skillfully, turned my raw manuscript into a book.

I must also offer thanks to Roger Ailes and Jack Reilly of CNBC who gave their permission and, indeed, their encouragement to pursue this project. In fact, they let me take a break from my daily "Traders' Tales" segment on CNBC to write this book.

To all I am quite indebted and forever grateful.

Author's Note

The tales in this storybook are all believed to be true, but it is safe to say that some are only apocryphal. In most instances, they are based on first-hand accounts from single sources. But there are also stories included in this tome that are memories, locked in the corners of some Wall Street minds, which may have tarnished a bit with age. So, some traders' tales may be exaggerated and some may be only partially accurate. However, in all cases the stories told to me depict, quite clearly, the flavor of the Street and the environment in which many investment professionals find themselves, for better or for worse.

RON INSANA

Fort Lee, New Jersey
March 1996

Contents

An Early Tale 1

First Corner, First Crash 1
The New York Stock Exchange 4

The Floor Trader 6

A Trader's Tail: The Bunny Suit 7
The $90,000 Mix-Up 11
Introducing Mitchell Mouse 12
The Silver Fox 14
Two Brooklyn Tales 15
Dead-Eye Corrigan 18
Hangovers and Heart Attacks 20
Reminiscences of a Stock Operator 22

Life in the Pits 28

Trading Soy Meal in Orlando 28
It's a Bear Market! 32
The $2,500 Cockroach 36
Leo the Lionhearted 40

The Trading Desk 49

Strung Out 50
Political Banter 53
PIMCO's Swinging Dick 55

Contents

Take Another Tick   58
Ticker Symbols   61

Women on Wall Street   65

The Queen of Wall Street   66
"Honey, You Can Get Right to It"   72
Abby Road   78

Greed, Gaming, and Trickery   82

Tall Tales   83
Gaming the Market   86
Free Willy   93
A Banker's Tale   96
A Trumped-Up Tale   99
Two No-Trump   103
Get It in Writing   106
Full Faith and Credit   109

Investors' Tales   114

Wall Street, Hollywood-Style   114
The Peter (Lynch) Principles   116
More About Magellan   121
The Sure Thing   127
Taxi . . .   131
Leon Cooperman   135
Short Takes   138
Investment Biker   145

Crash Tales   155

Crash Specialist   156
Timing Is Everything   159

Contents

Wang Lee   167
Few Options   171
Closing Rituals   173
An Author's Tale   175

Street Talk   179

The Predators' Ball   179
A Room With a View   181
The Bear   185
Gutter Ball   186

Constellations and Calendar Quirks   190

$igns of the Zodiac   190
A Little Lunacy   195
Quirks of the Calendar   197
Holy Holidays   200
The Super Bowl   203

Name Index   209

An Early Tale

Wall Street has always been the land of high-rollers, risk-takers, and risqué behavior. Because the Street is about money, its history has always been punctuated by booms and busts, by bull and bear markets, by greed and fear. Somewhere between those extremes the inhabitants of lower Manhattan have always found themselves precariously positioned. And oftentimes the pressure of living between the extremes makes them act as they do. It has ever been thus.

With that in mind, let us travel back to 1789, the year in which the United States of America was truly born. The constitutional convention now complete, Americans very eagerly set about the business of getting and spending, of building the economic dream that is cherished today.

First Corner, First Crash

In 1789 New York City was the nation's capital. At what is now the old Federal Building, a government was formed and a financial system was put into place. The proud and victorious players from the Revolution sprang into action.

Traders' Tales

The Constitution was enshrined, George Washington named first president and Alexander Hamilton, the first treasury secretary of the United States. From an economic standpoint, the task of building America appeared Herculean. The embryonic nation was buried beneath the debt incurred to finance the Revolutionary War. Lacking tax revenue, Secretary Hamilton scrambled to find a way to turn debt into equity, a strategy still employed by desperate governments today. He concocted the "Bank of the United States," a quasi-government entity that would allow debt holders to exchange their debt for a stake in the future of a fledgling country.

The nation's market for stocks and bonds was also embryonic. But with a long tradition for finance and commerce, the port of New York built a bustling market in securities even before the establishment of a formal exchange. On the streets of lower Manhattan, stockjobbers made markets in colonial war debt and in the equities of newly built banks, including the Bank of the United States. From here the tale becomes an all-too-familiar story of greed and conflict—traits that Wall Street tales would have in common for centuries to come.

One of Hamilton's most intimate associates was a man named William Duer, his assistant treasury secretary in 1789. Duer was a man of some repute, a semisuccessful speculator and a scion of New York's early establishment. He moved in and out of government jobs, trading places between government and finance with great speed.

William Duer was as avaricious a man as there was in government, frequently using his knowledge of government plans to his financial advantage. He speculated in bank stocks, cornered the market in some manufacturing

2

stocks, and according to one report, "was probably responsible for the advance notice which the creditor class had of the Hamiltonian financial program."* In other words, Duer passed along inside information to his closest friends. It would certainly not be the last time that a government official used his good offices to effect some financial gain.

Indeed, fully versed in the plan to convert colonial war debt into stock associated with the U.S. Bank, Duer embarked upon a grand scheme to corner the market in the existing securities in 1791. He hoped to make a killing on the conversion, once the government-led plan was put through.

He enlisted the help of one John Pintard, the founder of the New York Historical Society and the first full-time stockbroker on Wall Street. He was also one of Wall Street's earliest swindlers. Together they plotted to raise large sums of money from New York's middle-class inhabitants. Butchers, bakers, candlestick makers, even ladies of the evening, all lent Duer their hard-earned money. Pintard, a skilled stockjobber, traded hundreds and hundreds of presigned promissory notes to the eager lenders. The notes, signed by Duer, promised varying rates of interest—2, 3, even 5% interest, an astronomical sum for the time. Duer floated the first junk bonds on Wall Street. For all we know, his spirit may have taken the form of Michael Milken some 180 years later! The proceeds from his "debt offering" were sizable. Duer raised $697,517 in five months! Duer and a gang of prominent local businessmen attempted to use the pro-

---

*Source: J. Frese and J. Judd., eds., *Business Enterprise in Early New York*, Sleepy Hollow Press, p. 100.

ceeds to corner the market in a host of securities that comprised the embryonic stock market in early America. From mid-1791 to March of 1792, they speculated in bank stocks, floated rumors about pending mergers, and engaged in all the misdeeds that Wall Streeters would become famous for in later years. But their efforts failed miserably and eventually market forces overcame their ability to ramp up prices at the expense of public investors.

Like all market manipulations, this artificial corner failed. Duer, unable to drive the market to more profitable heights, was ruined financially by his escapades. He defaulted on his promissory notes, causing chaos among the townsfolk who had eagerly lent him money. There was a general panic in the financial sector as securities prices plummeted in March of 1792.

Riotous crowds sought out the conniving government official to extract their pound of flesh from the failed financier. But Duer, fearful for his life, threw himself in jail to avoid the lynch mobs that awaited him around lower Manhattan. The nation's first assistant treasury secretary was a wanted man—for starting the first financial panic in American history!

The New York Stock Exchange

In the wake of Wall Street's first crash, few, if any, of the market's early participants knew if they were still solvent. Trading activity ground to a halt from March until May. Finally, after much confusion and concern, twenty-four local stockbrokers gathered under a buttonwood tree in lower Manhattan and established a new stock market. Their efforts helped to revitalize a sagging market and to create what would become the largest stock market the world has ever seen.

The two dozen gentlemen, whose financial conditions were sound and their character (as far as we know) unimpeachable, signed the Buttonwood Accord, establishing the New York Stock & Exchange (NYS&E). They generated new rules for trading stocks and bonds, ensuring adequate capital and that fair commissions would be charged to NYS&E customers. In time, the NYS&E, borne out of a systemic panic, would become the preeminent financial institution in the world.

The Floor Trader

The floor of the New York Stock Exchange (NYSE) is the very center of capitalism's colorful universe. At its core, the floor traders and brokers are the market's atomic particles, constantly colliding into one another creating the heat and energy that power the economy. They are the quantum mechanics of the market, setting prices for securities and helping to raise capital for all types of economic endeavors.

These floor traders are about as busy as solar particles covering vast expanses of space and time. Veteran floor trader Art Cashin of PaineWebber says that on a slow day the average trader or broker walks two miles, on a busy day, five to six miles. All this action to match buyers and sellers and to set in motion the market forces that undergird America.

But traders and solar particles cease to be similar when it comes to character. Hydrogen atoms are, basically, all alike. When two collide, you get helium. And that's that. Ah, but traders are more like snowflakes—there are no two alike. Each brings a unique element to work every day, turning what could be a mundane exchange of money into a lively, picturesque display of capitalism.

It is here that we embark on a journey of the trading floor. From the NYSE to Chicago's commodity exchanges, we visit the characters of the floor, the traders whose tales are telling indeed.

A Trader's Tail: The Bunny Suit

Vic Sperandeo is a trader's trader. He'll trade anything from stocks to bonds to currencies to gold or cotton. Trader Vic has long been known as a hair-trigger type who loves to trade. Vic's an affable fellow who looks a bit like a Brooklyn-born wise guy. He's built like a bulldog, small but powerful. He's a gentle soul, though you can't quite tell that from looking at him. There's also a certain mischievousness in Trader Vic's eyes. One can tell from chatting with him that he knows a lot, some of which he probably could never tell you.

Vic's favorite story is "The Bunny Suit," a tale that illustrates the free-wheeling behavior that has long characterized many Wall Street players. They love a good joke, particularly at someone else's expense. Come to think of it, traders love anything that comes at someone else's expense. That's what makes 'em traders.

There used to be a bar in lower Manhattan that catered to the needs of Wall Street brokers and traders after the closing bell rang. It was a popular place where the weary unwound. The cozy atmosphere offered the perfect setting to relieve the stress of the day. Pressure often mounts for those who trade in money. Millions, sometimes billions, of dollars change hands on a busy day. This pressure makes traders do crazy things, if only to blow off steam.

It was here that all types of pressure could be relieved—a place where the male-dominated ranks of Wall Street could find comfort in the arms of a total stranger. At this uptown watering hole, Street workers met street walkers. The bar, as you've guessed by now, was also a place for working women, as well as legitimate, and attractive, professional women. The women of this place were quite discreet. In fact, oftentimes their own patrons never knew that some were working girls. In many cases, some of Wall Street's savviest traders simply thought they were doing quite well with the ladies.

As Vic Sperandeo tells it, one night some years ago a gentleman who shall remain nameless frequented the bar with some of his colleagues. They were tired from the maddening pace of the day, but not too tired for a stiff drink and a soft friend. The gentleman, well known to the locals, wore some pretty expensive accessories from a solid gold Rolex to gold rings—items that did not go unnoticed by the working inhabitants of the bar. Frequently the young turks of Wall Street, with plenty of fresh cash, looked for other conquests beyond the day's market victories.

After a grueling day, as the story goes, he decided to take the plunge into the night with one of the ladies. Although married and living in the suburbs, he frequently stayed in the city when work lasted too late or was going to begin too early. But, fortunately for our friend, he'd never have to explain this night to his wife. Only to his friends.

Ready for a little action, our trader friend took up with a lady of the evening. Alas for him, these girls were better versed at fleecing traders than some traders were at fleecing clients.

She "mickeyed" his drink before leaving the bar, and after he passed out at a nearby hotel, stole all his jewelry, his wallet, his clothes, and his shoes. As Vic tells it, these girls often took the additional precaution of stealing a john's clothes and shoes—in case he should wake up just after the crime. Quite often, the girls were able to resell the jewelry at a handsome profit. In many ways, it's hard to call them hookers, since very few of *these* girls ever slept with their customers. He slept. She didn't. When he awoke she was long gone.

When the trader awoke the next morning, he was bereft of his belongings. He was a naked short, as they say in trading parlance, meaning his position was fully exposed to maximum risk. Indeed, he could not head home to his wife to get clothes. Technically, he had nothing to hide, since he never actually committed adultery. Nonetheless, it might be hard to explain to his wife that had he not been drugged, knocked unconscious, and ripped off, he would have had a fling. Neither could he immediately go to work, where he was due on the floor of the New York Stock Exchange.

In desperation he called in to the office, begging his work associates to pay his hotel tab over the phone, send him a suit of clothes and cab fare as well. All of this they did. But much to his dismay, the suit of clothing did not consist of the usual jacket, pants, and tie. It was, instead, a big, white bunny suit, with large, floppy ears and a fluffy cotton tail.

He arrived at work on time, but was greeted at the door by a humorless security guard who tried to enforce Exchange rules that mandate a jacket and tie be worn on the floor. He argued that he was wearing a suit, albeit a bunny suit, and should be allowed on the floor. The guard relented and he headed to his post on the floor. Ultimately his friends took pity on him and bought him a more proper suit of clothes.

THE BUNNY SUIT

To this day, floor traders talk of the time when a bunny visited Wall Street after having quite clearly laid an egg elsewhere.

[Other versions of this story claim the trader never took up with a prostitute but instead was simply so drunk when he went to his hotel that he climbed into a cold shower, clothes and all, in an effort to revive himself from a most brutal inebriation. In the morning, he couldn't find his clothing, lumped, as it was, in a corner of the bathroom, hidden behind the door. From that point on the story is the same. Eyewitnesses saw our man on the exchange floor in a bunny suit the following day. They have testified to it. That much we know is true.]

The $90,000 Mix-Up

In the 1950s, Wall Street was run by John Coleman. He was a devout Catholic, a special papal chamberlain, no less. He was said to run the city of New York—a key third of a governing troika consisting of Coleman, Cardinal Spellman, and Mayor Wagner. Coleman was feared by some, hated by others, but he was among the most powerful men ever to work on Wall Street.

Bob Scavone, a veteran specialist on the floor of the New York Stock Exchange, remembers Coleman's proud ways. He was "divine" on Wall Street, having been born on December 24 and having the initials J. C., Coleman's word was law. Unfortunately for Coleman, his power was so great that one of his own commands cost him a small fortune.

Back then food and drink were forbidden on the floor of the Big Board. Liquids were considered a particular hazard, because someone could slip on spilled fluids in the rush to do business.

Now Coleman's son-in-law worked for his firm and frequently ignored market etiquette. He would sneak a soft drink down to the floor and hide it carefully behind the specialist post. It just so happened that Coleman's firm made a market in Coke of New York, a Coca-Cola bottling concern that no longer exists. Bob Scavone and Al Smith recall that Coleman held a position in Coke of New York, totalling some 80,000–90,000 shares. The position for the firm's account was a large stock holding in its day. As Scavone and Smith tell it, Coleman felt the bottling concern would one day be taken over, and his large stake in Coke of New York would eventually jump in value.

11

One day J. C. spotted an open can of Coke at his son-in-law's foot.

"Get rid of the Coke," he barked, failing to explicitly point at the can of soda.

The boy, eager to do the old man's bidding, or at least avoid his wrath, yelled out: "I've got 90,000 Coke for sale." A willing buyer snapped up the 90,000 shares in an instant. The son-in-law managed to dump the entire stake, quickly and fearlessly, the hallmark of a good trader.

According to the lore of the floor, the next day Coke of New York went up a dollar, immediately costing Coleman $90,000 in lost profits.

His son-in-law was never caught with a Coke can again.

Introducing Mitchell Mouse

Laura Pederson is a former trader on the floor of the American Stock Exchange. The AMEX, or "curb" as it is commonly known, is the smaller of New York's stock exchanges, by far. The curb literally began as a curbside exchange where brokers did business whenever the Big Board shut its doors. The longest shutdown in the history of the NYSE occurred in 1914 at the outbreak of World War I. The Big Board halted trading for six months. During that period brokers traded curbside in an effort to do business. Eventually, the curbside activity was brought indoors and the American Stock Exchange was born.

Laura Pederson traded options at the AMEX and was so successful that she made a million dollars by the time she was twenty-one. She quit the business, wrote a book called *Play Money*, and now writes a personal finance column for the *New York Times*.

As Pederson recalls, floor traders are a superstitious lot. They are like athletes in that respect. Like competitive sports, on any given day the market can go against you. So traders, like athletes, want a competitive advantage when it comes to winning on Wall Street. Some carry lucky key chains. Others wear lucky clothes. This is the story of an AMEX floor trader who kept a lucky mouse, a little rubber mouse that brought him good luck in one particular stock.

The trader made a market in shares of Mitchell Development Corporation, an energy services company that has traded on the curb for years. The company's mascot, for some unknown reason, was a mouse, Mitchell Mouse. The company frequently gave away little rubber Mitchells to anyone who wanted one.

Well, Mitchell Development's specialist surely wanted one, and he kept it at his specialist post at all times. This superstitious specialist used to rub Mitchell Mouse's head every time he wanted, or needed, the stock to go up. Worked for *him*.

One day, the specialist came to work only to find Mitchell Mouse was missing. In his place was a note that read as follows: "If you ever want to see Mitchell alive again, leave $200 with the guard downstairs."

The specialist, bent but not bowed, decided not to play along, assuming the stunt was the harmless prank of one of his playful floor brethren.

He was wrong. The next day, another note. He still did not respond.

On the following day, Mitchell's ear was left at the specialist's post, with another note pushing the ransom to $500!

The next day, Mitchell's arm was delivered. The specialist began to sweat. His lucky charm was coming back to him in pieces, leaving very little to rub on bad market days.

He finally paid the $500 ransom. Mitchell was returned. After a little cosmetic surgery he was as good as new. The specialist never was.

The Silver Fox

Wall Street has had its share of "silver foxes." Many of the Street's old-timers were accorded such an affectionate moniker, respectful of their reputations as grizzled veterans of Wall Street's many hunts. The foxes were always the wily ones on Wall Street and they generally passed their wisdom on to the younger members of the brood, leaving behind their legacies as the most cunning players the floor has ever seen. Despite the respect generally reserved for the aging traders, the younger players often targeted them when a little levity was required.

One of the favorite pranks perpetrated by the Big Board's younger set involved attacking a silver fox where he lived—on the trading floor. One particular silver fox, who spent many years of his life on the floor of the stock exchange, had seen and done it all. He worked the floors for decades, darting about, executing trades, and doing deals for his customers with lightning speed and traversing the floor of the Big Board countless times in his many years as a floor trader.

But in his later years it became tougher for him to maintain the frantic pace. By the 1960s he was tiring of the walk and required the use of a cane. A proud man with an air of civility he used a shiny, ebony bar, capped by a silver headpiece, and rounded out by a vinyl tip. But even this revered old trader was not spared the practical jokes of the exchange's more youthful players. One of the younger set decided to secretly whittle away at the Fox's cane, shaving off small amounts from the end of the big black stick and replacing the vinyl tip at the bottom when the whittling was done. The whittling went on for weeks, as imperceptible amounts were shaved off, a little at a time. The Silver Fox never noticed, even though over the course of several weeks he began to hunch over a little more each day in an effort to use his walking aid.

After about nine weeks, 6 inches of cane were whittled away, and the Silver Fox was walking more like Igor in a Frankenstein movie than the proud man of stature that he was at the NYSE.

At the end of nine weeks, someone asked the Fox what was the matter with his gait.

"Must be my back."

Two Brooklyn Tales

The Revlon Truck

It's tough to get started on Wall Street. Even those with the best degrees, the most remarkable pedigrees, or just the necessary raw intelligence often have a difficult time breaking into the financial district network. But there are many ways to gain entry to the Street. The front door, the back door, even the side doors to Wall Street let in the players with the drive and the guts to master the game.

And so goes the story of a young man who took an alternative route. We'll call him Vinnie. This young fellow grew up on the mean streets of Brooklyn. He was "environmentally influenced." Not that Vinnie was a hood, but back in Brooklyn in the 1960s, it was tough not to come across a wise guy or two. And Vinnie was clearly looking to live the easy life—just like some of the local boys who made good by doing bad.

One day Vinnie and a friend decided to knock off a Revlon truck. The big cosmetics truck delivered lipstick and makeup to local retailers. They planned the heist on their own, so the story goes. It wasn't a mob deal. It was just two young guys, "making their bones" because they had little else going for them. They wired the truck while the driver was eating in a diner and made away with a rather sizable cache of lipstick and lotions.

But even in Brooklyn in the 1960s it wasn't all that easy to fence a seemingly inexhaustible supply of cosmetics without getting nabbed by the cops or "protected" by the neighborhood big shot. So Vinnie and his friend devised a plan to sell the stolen goods.

Each got a job on Wall Street. Wall Street firms have always been populous places: lots of traders and lots of secretaries, all making comparatively good money and all with a taste for quality goods.

So Vinnie landed an entry-level job at a major brokerage house and started selling his wares. Lipsticks were flying out of his hands at $2, $3, or $4 apiece. His friend was doing the same. For an entire year, they made about an extra $100 a day—about $25,000 a year. In the 1960s, $25,000 was some pretty good scratch for two young entrepreneurs from Brooklyn. They were making a great base salary on the Street and a bonus override from Revlon.

Eventually, though, the contraband was depleted. Vinnie, ironically enough, found life on Wall Street as exciting as life on the mean streets. He stayed there for two decades, earning a living as a trader in over-the-counter stocks. He might have even traded Revlon, just for kicks, who knows?

One source says Vinnie is on welfare today. The last firm he traded with went bankrupt in the crash of '87. It seems the firm he worked for engaged in some sort of securities fraud.

You can take the boy out of Brooklyn, but you can't always take Brooklyn out of the boy.

Brooklyn Savior

Vic Sperandeo recalls the story of another young Brooklyn boy who desperately wanted to make his fortune on Wall Street. As Vic tells it, this young boy needed about $25,000 to stake his claim in the world of Wall Street's high rollers. But he was of modest means, lacking the financial wherewithal to shepherd that kind of cash, so, intent on getting into the trading business, he visited what Vic calls a "Brooklyn Savior." A loan shark is the more common term.

In the basement of the savior's home, the young man asked for a loan—twenty-five grand to make his way. The savior acted as any hometown savior would and loaned the boy $25,000 on the spot. The young man, still in his early twenties, brimming with the unguarded optimism of youth, thanked his savior, telling him he would have no problem paying the money back.

Saviors are wonderful people, as religion tells us. They help us in times of trouble and teach the lessons we need to learn. In this case, our boy got the benefit of both some help and some education. Our savior led the boy over to a basement freezer. Instructing the boy to look closely, he pulled out an ice block and wiped away the frosty shavings that obscured the object frozen inside. It was a hand. The savior pointed out to our optimistic young trader that the last borrower who promised not to be a problem failed to pay back the money he owed. Now, while the savior took the boy at his word, he also wanted to offer one of life's lessons on prompt payment.

"This guy was not a problem," the savior warned. "He borrowed some money. Never paid it back."

On Wall Street, they call the rate of interest charged to investors the "broker loan rate." In Brooklyn it's the severed hand rate. And needless to say, the young man never lost any money trading in his early days. He doesn't trade for a living any more, but he did manage to pay his savior back as promised.

True story, Vic promised.

Dead-Eye Corrigan

Dead-Eye Corrigan was so named because one of his eyes was gone. In its place was an eye made of glass.

The Floor Trader

Dead-Eye was quite fond of glass, particularly the kind that would hold liquor. He was a big drinker, needless to say.

As the story goes, Dead-Eye got polluted one night in New York City, after a long day's work on the floor of the Exchange. He was so smashed that he somehow lost his glass eye in a drunken stupor. The next morning, hung over and visually challenged, Dead-Eye stalked around the room looking for his eye. The eye was nowhere to be found. He was due at the Big Board shortly and decided to explore the next available option.

Dead-Eye rushed to a local drug store to buy a patch to cover the hole where his glass eye once was.

He hurriedly inquired about the availability of eye patches from the woman behind the counter.

"Do you carry eye patches?" he asked the clerk.

"How many do you need, sir?" she inquired.

An agitated Dead-Eye responded, "Lady, if I needed two, I'd get a damn Seeing Eye dog."

She sold him one patch. He headed to work at the Big Board, patch in place, but clearly, short one eye. The locals on the floor were unsympathetic to Dead-Eye's plight. They were quite familiar with his binges, but this one took the cake.

One of the floor brokers sneaked out during the day to purchase a few hundred Superballs—those ultra-bouncy balls so popular in the late '60s and early '70s. Each had an eye imprinted on it, giving the bouncy balls the eerie impression of being disembodied visual apparatus.

Around two o'clock, several hundred floor traders began bouncing the eye balls on the floor in unison, in tribute to Dead-Eye's missing lens. Immediately thereafter, a cake with a bloodshot eye frosted on top was delivered to Dead-Eye.

AT 2:00, TRADERS BEGAN BOUNCING SUPERBALLS

Hangovers and Heart Attacks

In the 1970s, the membership of the New York Stock Exchange was graying a bit around the temples. Old-timers, remnants from bygone days, dominated Wall Street. These veterans had seen a host of events, some dating back to the Roaring Twenties and others, while not quite as old, could tell you clearly how bad the depression really was or what World War II was really like. Al Smith recalls the early 1970s, when he first set foot on the Exchange. The Big Board was nearly an infirmary for floor traders.

As in most rest homes, there were bound to be a few instances in which health problems arose. It wasn't unusual for the membership to nap a little extra in the lounge, or for some traders to miss extra days, or maybe even stop showing up altogether. That happens when players in an institution begin to age.

Smith remembers one old-timer who had stretched out on a couch in the member's lounge one morning and never awoke. The old boy had a heart attack, turned blue, and died right on the sofa. At first no one in the lounge realized the old man had actually died. Some of the younger members of the exchange called emergency assistance and pleaded for help. Twenty-odd years ago, the Exchange was not outfitted with a medical staff as it is now.

The concerned callers frantically told the medics about their colleague who had apparently suffered cardiac arrest. They said they feared he might already be dead, given the rather blue tint to his aged skin.

Coincidentally in that very same room, a friend of Smith's was a bit blue as well. He too was laid out on a sofa suffering the ill effects of a terrible hangover. He was unaware of the happenings around him. Before he slept though, he had swallowed some antacid tablets to calm his jittery stomach and hopefully ease the intense pounding in his head.

As Al's friend slept off his hangover, the medics burst through the door, looking for the victim. Spotting an ashen face and limp body, they rushed to Smith's friend, quickly sizing up the extent of the emergency. The collection of a chalky white substance in the corner of his mouth confirmed their worst fears: The patient was near death. Immediately, they began pounding on the stricken man's chest in a desperate attempt to restart his failing heart. It was the wrong guy. Al's friend woke up screaming, with the pain in his ribs now equalling the one in his badly hung-over head.

Reminiscences of a Stock Operator

Michael Metrenko is eighty-six years old. He is the old-est trader with a seat on the floor of the New York Stock Exchange. Today his comfortable life is a far cry from his early years as a saloonkeeper's son in the mining town of Scranton, Pennsylvania. Metrenko and his family own stocks that he estimates will be worth about $100 million in another ten years. The barkeep's son has done all right for himself.

Metrenko is intimately familiar with the games that are played in the market. He has seen them all, from the "gaming" that occurred a few short years ago, to episodes of "painting the tape," and to the outright manipulations of the market by the investment polls of the Roaring Twenties. Indeed, Michael got his start on Wall Street in 1928.

In 1928, Wall Street enjoyed one of its wildest years. The economy was booming, stock prices were soaring, and the Roaring Twenties were in full swing. The Dow Jones industrial average was vaulting to unheard of heights as the lords of Wall Street and the denizens of Main Street chased stocks to loftier and loftier levels. John J. Raskob, the noted financier who would one day head the Democratic National Party, wrote that if all Americans would just invest $10,000 a year in good common stocks, each and every citizen could be rich. A heady notion for a heady time. It proved to be a miserably inaccurate forecast of what was to come.

Few people noticed the impending signs of danger in the America of the 1920s—the bust of the Florida real estate boom, the slowdown in economic activity, the trade tensions that were growing daily around the world. The giddiness of the easy life itself may have been the surest sign that life in America was a bit too good to be true. It would all come to a crashing end in October of 1929.

Metrenko, a good Catholic boy of Russian extraction, began his life's work as a page boy on the floor of the New York Stock Exchange in 1928, running tickets back and forth across the floor for the big boys who dominated the Street. Pulling down a princely sum of $15 a week, Metrenko was lucky to have escaped Scranton, a dingy coal-mining town where men died where they worked, in the freezing, dark shafts hundreds of feet below ground.

Metrenko himself worked in a saloon, which was a far cry better than the cold and unwelcoming bowels of the earth. After one look down a mine shaft, Metrenko, who dreamed of a better life, decided to make his way to the Street, giving up his familiar, but uncomfortable, life in Scranton.

Metrenko started on Wall Street when the likes of J.P. Morgan and Bernard Baruch were on their way to becoming legends. The fabled trader Jesse Livermore did business on the floor of the NYSE—and Metrenko had seen him trade. Chrissy Hanson, Larry Oakley, and Ray Bond were three of the fabled Morgan brokers. The big boys who, when they had business to do, traded in chunks of 50,000 to 100,000 shares, the most awesome transactions anyone had ever seen. It was then that Metrenko learned the game that never changes.

His mentor was Frank E. Bliss, from Newport, North Carolina. By 1928 Bliss was a legend on the floor. They called him the Silver Fox. The blissful Bliss and a partner raked in $12 million that year from trading in stocks, a sum that is huge today, let alone back then.

The Silver Fox taught him how to execute a trade and how to set up the crowd. The art of painting the tape was a useful method of distributing stock that is sometimes still used today, but not nearly as well or as frequently as it was in the Roaring Twenties. The setup was always quite simple, and it always required the participation of one of those folks, who as P. T. Barnum once said, "was born every minute."

Painting the tape (or gaming the market) makes the activity in a particular stock look so good that one just has to get in on the action. A player and his comrades used to generate a little action in a stock by bidding up its price, buying and selling the stock back and forth among one another. Then they'd put the word out that the action in a stock was "hot." Eventually other players would come to the post where the stock traded and start buying. They'd get their clients in while the original players would unload their holdings to the newly interested crowd. It was a put-up job.

Frank E. Bliss was a master at working the crowd and in painting the tape. Metrenko recalls one of the most masterful painting jobs Bliss engineered many, many years ago.

Since the early part of this century, a famous meat packing company was a recognized name in packaged hams and other meat products, such as Spam. It was well known on Wall Street as well. Its stock traded on the Big Board for years, back into the 1920s.

The Floor Trader

Metrenko remembers a big block of the company's stock was up for sale back in the late 1920s. One of the premier brokers on the Street, Eastman Dillon, was putting a million shares of the firm out on behalf of the company. Dillon had one of his brokers begin parceling the shares out to willing buyers. But the broker, lacking any skill in making the meat company's stock more tantalizing, botched the job.

The point of unloading any stock is to sell it at the best possible price for the seller, even if the size of the block would naturally depress the price. But a skilled broker worth his salt would never let the size of the sale unduly depress the price of the stock. Eastman Dillon's man failed miserably at that task, selling the first 25,000 shares down a dollar and a quarter. The executives at the company were not pleased. If 25,000 shares knocked the stock down more than a buck, what would a million shares do?

The Silver Fox was a legend for his ability to generate interest in a stock, so Eastman Dillon called him in to handle the deal.

"Frank, we have an order here to sell a million shares, and we put it down to the floor, and they botched it up. Now, that's not the way to do a stock."

"I would think not," Frank said rather matter-of-factly.

"We're counting on you. We're going to give you the order tomorrow and let you do the job."

The Silver Fox and Mike Metrenko arrived at work a little early that morning, ready to do some serious business. The Fox began selling some stock lightly, eventually parceling out 50,000 shares. The stock moved down a half dollar. At that point, three big position players who already owned a lot of the stock took some of it off the Fox's hands. Four other hand-selected men worked their way into the crowd, and, on cue, lightly bid up the price of the stock, making sure to tell other brokers that the action in the meat packer was looking good. They make phone calls, saying "Hey, this stock looks right. It's acting well. You should buy some."

Needless to say the stock was distributed with minimal price impact. It took the Silver Fox a few days to unload the remaining 975,000 shares. But with his skill at painting the tape, the unloading of that parcel never pushed the stock down more than a dollar and a quarter, the same amount it dropped when only 25,000 shares were sold by a less skilled market mechanic. Metrenko says stock is distributed the same way today. The stock pools back in the 1920s worked the crowd constantly, generating the action, letting the price drift up, enticing buyers through some strong word of mouth advertising, and then selling out the other side. Nifty little way to make money, trading stocks.

Mike's Moonlighting

Michael Metrenko made a lot of money trading and investing in stocks. But some of his best remembrances are of the days when he did a little moonlighting on the floor of the Exchange.

The money from working the floor was uneven at best, particularly after the 1929 crash. Metrenko made extra by directing business to certain brokers. They'd tip him to keep them up to date on the important order flow of the day. It paid to know what was going on from specialist post to specialist post.

The Floor Trader

That was the routine business of the day back then. But Metrenko also earned supplemental income from selling everything from men's socks to women's stockings on the floor of the Exchange. He would pick up hose wholesale all over New York and resell it on the floor. Some years he made more money selling hose than he did selling stocks. Traders and brokers have always been an enterprising bunch.

Metrenko's best sideline came from the side bets that he generated on college football. Metrenko knew all types of people in New York. Some were well heeled and well respected; others only got their names in the papers for less acceptable reasons. But Metrenko knew them all.

In the mid 1960s, when New York was home to more than a few wise guys, Metrenko and a pal decided to start a betting pool on college football. They put up $20 apiece to begin operations and sent betting cards to college campuses all over the Northeast. Students at Penn State, University of Pennsylvania, and even Cornell, played the game, which netted Metrenko $4,400 in the first year alone.

By the time the game had grown to its potential size, Mike was making $150,000 from the pool alone, more money than he was making in the stock market!

But some of the local boys, whose names end in vowels, heard about this profitable little enterprise. They called Mike in and asked for a piece of the action. So Michael, very willingly, gave a 100% piece. That was his last effort at moonlighting. But he lived to trade another day—and that's all any trader really wants.

Life in the Pits

In Chicago there are the trading pits. They exist in the commodity exchanges on LaSalle Street, in the heart of the Windy City's financial district. Futures pits on the floor of the Chicago exchanges are the areas in which a host of commodities from soybeans to pork bellies are bought and sold.

The pits have often been even more freewheeling places than the trading floors of the more subdued East Coast. The New York Stock Exchange floor, for all its history of wild behavior and locker-room talk is nothing when compared to the Chicago futures pits. In the pits, the zaniest market rumors get started. In the pits, polar bears get punched and cockroaches get eaten. The pits can be like one big frat party, while the NYSE floor is more like a men's dormitory. A subtle difference, to be sure, but the differences will become more clear in the following few pages.

Trading Soy Meal in Orlando

Trading can be a compulsion, just like gambling. Some traders simply can't give up the action. They can't stop to do other things. They *have* to trade. It can be an addiction. They might be addicted to learning more and more about the economic world around them, they might be addicted to excitement, they might be addicted to the money or just the joy of winning. Whatever the reason, there are some pretty compulsive traders out there who just can't stop, not even while on vacation.

John Wicker* made his money trading soy meal, one of three commodities that makes up what's known in the Chicago trading pits as the "soy complex." Soybeans, soy oil, and soy meal are widely used commodities that feed people and livestock around the world. From soy burgers to cattle feed, nearly everyone in the world encounters the soy complex at some point in life. And like other agricultural commodities, whether it's corn or wheat or oats, cattle, pork bellies, or orange juice, these commodities not only are bought and sold in the physical sense among producers of goods and consumers of products, they are also traded in the Chicago commodity pits. This free trade allows commodity speculators to bet on the weather, the size of the corn crop, the health of the cattle market, or in this case, the supply and demand for soy meal.

John Wicker spent a lot of his young life grinding a living out in the soy meal pit. It's a place that houses true bean counters. The size and quality of the crop are the biggest determinants of its price come harvest time, so everyone from farmers to hedge fund speculators track everything from planting to flowering to harvesting. And

---

*John Wicker is a real person but his name has been changed here at his request.

they watch the weather. They watch all the grain markets, in fact, where buyers and sellers meet from all over the world to purchase the stuff that will feed their people.

Grain and bean traders are a quirky lot. They use some arcane charts that show the trading patterns of various commodities over the course of time. With those complicated factors rushing through their heads at all moments of the day, soy meal traders buy and sell futures contracts, betting on the direction of soy meal prices, hoping to earn enough money speculating on food prices to feed their families at home.

Trading in the Chicago futures pits for oneself is a crushing experience. One must be attentive to all aspects of this market at all times, not only to capitalize on the potential profits in the pits, but also to avoid the pitfalls themselves. A single mistake can wipe out an individual trader. A great trade can make a speculator rich.

John Wicker fell somewhere in between. As a young soymeal trader in the 1970s, Wicker was a bit addicted to the trade. He was not a big speculator. He was what they call in the business "a local." He lived in Chicago and went to work at the Board of Trade, trading soy meal futures contracts for a living. He was a local as opposed to a big grain house (producer) who also trades grain futures contracts. He was a local as opposed to a big hedge-fund speculator (fund) who dabbles in these derivatives. And he was a local compared to big New York brokerage firms (commission houses) who are also responsible for moving the grain markets from time to time.

Wicker was a local. He never held onto a trade overnight. An unexpected burst of rain could wipe out his capital if he was betting the wrong way the day before. He never wanted to be exposed to any condition that he couldn't immediately trade into or trade away from. That was his rule.

Until 1978. John Wicker's wife had had just about enough of his working himself to death. He was only a young man, but he was consumed by the trading life. At one point, she finally demanded he take a vacation. And while on vacation, he could not trade. Wicker finally agreed. But John Wicker was a superstitious man who felt an instinctual need to trade. So before departing for a Disney World vacation, he put in an order unbeknownst to his wife.

He used his lucky number and put in an order to buy eleven soy meal futures contracts. He left orders with his broker to buy contracts as they declined in price. The market had been under some pressure as he was leaving and he felt no need to buy the contracts at the top of what was likely to be a quick move downward. He got on the plane and tried to forget about the trade so he could finally relax and enjoy his young family and some time off.

But one night was all Wicker could take of peace and quiet. While strolling through the Magic Kingdom in Orlando, Wicker was seized with an urge to check what had happened. He ducked into a restroom and called his broker in Chicago.

The meal market had collapsed before Wicker's orders were put through and it was his good fortune that the broker bought his eleven contracts at very reasonable prices. He caught the bottom of the move. Wicker grew a bit anxious about his trades and frequently went into the Mickey's room several more times, always coming out grinning. His wife was perplexed by his joyous trips to the loo. But he explained that he simply had too many sodas that day. She never questioned his story.

The next day the pattern continued. Into the restroom, out with a smile. The soy meal market moved up its allowable limit on Wicker's second vacation day. He made $75,000 in profits in less than forty-eight hours. He was quite refreshed and relaxed on his long-awaited vacation.

His wife thought he should vacation more often.

It's a Bear Market!

There are bear markets and then there are *bear markets*. For the uninitiated, a bear market is a market (for any type of investment) in which prices generally fall. Stocks, bonds, and commodities all suffer bear markets from time to time. Some are like little brown bears, dangerous only when one gets too close. Others are like great big, ferocious grizzlies that maul anyone or anything in sight, costing investors countless dollars and investment professionals their jobs.

The 1990 bear market in stocks was a little brown bear. It was cute as far as bear markets go. The 1920s bear market in stocks was a grizzly. There was nothing cute about this at all. The bear market in the 1920s ushered in the Great Depression and economic calamity for an entire nation.

Then there are polar bear markets. This is a bear market that has occurred only once in market history. It occurred in Chicago, in August of 1994. This bear was neither cute nor savage. And it only cost one job, the job of a trader on the floor of the Chicago Board of Trade (CBOT).

The CBOT, or simply, the Board, is a place where commodity futures are traded. At the very end of LaSalle Street in the Windy City sits a cold, stone building that houses the oldest futures exchange in the country. Since its early days, the Board allowed farmers to hedge their exposure to the vicissitudes of planting crops by allowing the growers of goods to buy and sell commodity futures—contracts that allowed the farmers to lock in prices for their goods long before the final harvest. The futures contracts guaranteed the farmers some income, should their crops be unexpectedly large, which would drive down prices, or unexpectedly small, which would drive up prices but scare away buyers.

That was the original purpose of the Board of Trade. Today it still provides that service, although the farmers are mostly huge agribusinesses that both hedge against losses in their crops and also speculate on what the size and price of a certain crop might ultimately be. In addition to commodity futures, financial futures on bonds and currencies are also traded at the CBOT. Portfolio managers who buy and sell bonds or currencies use the Board's products to hedge against the natural disasters that sometimes strike their markets as well.

Since its establishment in the 1800s, the Board has seen countless bull and bear markets, in everything from soybeans to cattle or from pork bellies to U.S. bonds. But until August of 1994, no one on the floor had ever seen a bear market like this. Traders say this particular "bear trap" came from right out of the blue. But it was savage in its implications.

The action at the Chicago Board of Trade was routine on this August morning in 1994. A trader, whom we'll call Larry, was having a good morning, preparing for another day in the Chicago futures pits. Larry visited his fellow traders, shared some jokes, and checked his investment positions in the market, all before grabbing a bite to eat off the floor. He rambled about the bustling Board of Trade floor, doing his business, placing his bets, making his trades. While he was careful to avoid a nasty bear market that had ravaged bond investments in 1994, he stepped right into another bear—the bear from the Brookfield Zoo.

The zoo had launched a major promotional campaign in August of 1994 to raise money for the care and feeding of its happy inhabitants. One such effort was sending a polar bear to the Chicago Board of Trade. Not a real polar bear, but a young Chicago student dressed as one. He was making a few bucks drumming up donations for his brothers behind bars.

Larry was on his way to breakfast when he first encountered the bear. It was a quiet morning as we said, and floor traders, being a restless lot, always look for ways to spice up the day when the markets aren't providing the required adrenaline rush. So to kill a little time and just for a few laughs, a pal of Larry's challenged him to an early morning bet, a challenge no floor trader can ever resist.

Floor traders spend their lives betting. Betting on bull markets, betting on bear markets, betting on the direction of everything from soybean prices to interest rates, so it's rare that they ever just say no to a gamble.

"I'll bet you ten bucks you don't go up and smack that bear on the snout," Larry's buddy said.

"Make it $25 and I'll do it. But I'll give the money to the zoo. It's a good cause."

The gauntlet thrown, Larry made his way over to the Brookfield bear, chatted with him briefly, told him about his little bet, and then slapped him on the snout. The bear was a bit stunned by the blow, or at least so he later claimed.

Life in the Pits

For some reason the bear was not amused by Larry's little prank. In fact, the polar bear pulled his own head off and cried foul, claiming that tap really hurt and worse, pushed his glasses into his face, bruising his real nose.

For a moment there was a tense standoff between Larry and the bear. But after a few moments, the bear accepted Larry's apology and went on shilling for the Brookfield Zoo.

Larry, meantime, headed off for a little breakfast with his pals—a chastened man for having wrestled with a bear and lost. As far as Larry was concerned, he and the bear were square. But by the time Larry returned from his morning meal, the trading floor was abuzz with the amazing tale of a polar bear that was mauled by a floor trader. In the short time that Larry was away, the story had taken on a life all its own. It grew to a grizzly-sized story.

Word had it that the bear was coldcocked and taken away by ambulance. Paramedics resuscitated the bear and took him to the hospital for observation. And Larry, one of the many arrogant, immature floor traders, was to blame for sending the bear into an unseasonable hibernation.

It wasn't long before various news services carried *that* story on the ticker tape, describing the scene as it was told, not as it actually occurred. A day later, the story ran in the *Chicago Sun-Times* and it played on local radio stations. It was a man bites dog story that never took place.

As the story grew, Larry's bosses grew concerned. Board of Trade officials fretted over the bad press that was building day by day, characterizing floor traders as a lawless bunch who rarely abide by rules and frequently make mischief rather than money.

Because of all the negative publicity, Larry lost his job. He was fired and has since found a new job. His friends are sensitive to his plight, refusing to divulge his name for fear that Larry will be hounded further by his brush with the bear.

The $2,500 Cockroach

If you've never seen the floor of a major futures exchange in Chicago, it's hard to envision. Thousands of traders and brokers packed into cramped spaces, yelling and screaming at each other, placing million dollar bets in a blur of hand signals or finger wiggles amid a deafening din that would make airport runway workers cover their ears. On a busy day in the pits, there is nothing but a sea of humanity pushing, shoving, gesturing—sometimes obscenely—all in an effort to execute a trade. It can be a most unseemly way to make a living.

By the same token, being a trader can be like being a cop: For every tense, action-packed minute, there is an hour of just milling about, waiting for something to happen. The trading floor can get eerily quiet, just like a rain-soaked city street around midnight.

But there is always the *potential* for action and that's what makes the game worth playing for those who ply the trading trade. In those moments of *potential action*, traders often look for any type of activity to break the monotony. Whether it's fraternal horsing around, joke-telling or story-telling, traders are notorious for finding ways to fill the empty moments.

A few years back, one unusually quiet moment produced a tale still told on the floor of the Board of Trade.

Life in the Pits

It happened in the ten-year note pit. Ten-year treasury notes, like the benchmark thirty-year bonds, are debt obligations of the U.S. government. In Chicago, the Board of Trade has a trading pit dedicated to ten-year note futures, giving large investors a chance to hedge their holding of ten-year notes through the buying and selling of futures contracts. Big and small investors like to invest in ten-year notes because their interest rate payments are usually quite generous and they don't tie up their money for nearly as long as investing in a thirty-year bond.

Like all sorts of bonds, the ten-year note's price and yield are influenced by events taking place in the economy. If the economy is growing slowly without inflation, the price of the note will rise and the yield will fall, because investors feel confident that economic growth is not so strong that it will produce inflation. Inflation eats away at the purchasing power of bond investments. That's because there's no guaranty that when the note matures the returned principal will have as much purchasing power as it did when the investment was first made. Conversely, strong growth and rising inflation drive down the price of the note and drive up the yield. Investors clamor for a higher yielding bond when inflation ravages the purchasing power of fixed income investments. And like the thirty-year bond, the ten-year note trades violently when the economic news of the day drastically alters the perceptions of investors as to the pace of economic growth, the level of inflation and ultimately, the direction of interest rates.

But the violent action does not occur every day. And when it's dull in the pits, life, itself, is the pits. One painfully dull day several years back, a cockroach scurried across the floor of the Board, freed by some construction workers who had been repairing the walls of the ancient exchange. The newly liberated vermin darted across the highly populated floor, dodging the soles of the few active traders who, sometimes like bugs themselves, scamper across the hardwood floor in search of business. This unlucky cockroach did manage to avoid the crush of feet and a most humiliating, but common, extermination. But unhappily for this refugee from the roach motel, a more cruel fate awaited him. He was eventually captured by a bored bond trader who was looking for a little action.

The cockroach, like the "Cricket in Times Square," was about to provide all the action the floor would see that day. It quickly became the object of a high-priced prank. A pot of $2,500 was quickly raised by a gathering group of traders and set aside for any floorwalker who would consume the cockroach—a goldfish-eating prank that just might lighten things up at the boring Board of Trade.

A hapless young clerk in the ten-year note pit, a fresh-faced, underpaid gopher eager for some adulation and for something to do, took the bait. A carnival crowd quickly gathered around the young man, whose paltry clerk's salary did little to support his emerging taste for the good life. Soon a hush fell over the entire floor as the starving artisan prepared to down the roach, which he did with great aplomb.

The crowd let out a collective groan and a chorus of "Ohhhh, God, he did it," rose from the ranks.

The clerk pocketed the $2,500, queasy but thankful for the hard-earned bonus. He just received a 15% pay increase for a college prank. He, like the others around him, was quite amused. However, a security guard on the floor of the Exchange was not. Now, as the tale goes, the guard witnessed the entire event, from the collection of the funds to the consummation of the deal, so to speak. He let the whole thing happen. But when the clerk's digestive juices began flowing, the guard put his foot down.

The humorless guard began writing citations for the clerk's behavior, fining him for obstructing trading and eating on the floor, both of which are forbidden by CBOT rules. Needless to say, the fines are in excess of, you guessed it, $2,500. Unfortunately for the clerk, the broker he worked for was pinched for the rest of the dough.

The enterprising young clerk lost the $2,500 bonus and his job.

THE $2,500 COCKROACH

Leo the Lionhearted

L eo Melamed is the chairman emeritus of the Chicago Mercantile Exchange. He is a legend in the city of big shoulders for creating the market for futures on financial assets nearly singlehandedly. Leo championed the development of stock index futures—derivative contracts that are used as proxies for stock market indexes. They allow investors to buy or sell futures contracts at a fraction of what it costs to buy the underlying basket of stocks. Financial futures, like commodity futures, allow investors to hedge, or offset, the risks associated with holding large baskets of common stocks. The futures markets also allow speculators to buy and sell stock equivalents quickly and easily, without ever having to own the stocks outright.

Before he became the chairman of the Chicago Mercantile Exchange, where stock index futures are traded, Melamed was a trader himself. In fact, he remained a trader even after he ran the exchange—a potential conflict that could have hurt him in the crash of '87. But he was able to dodge a pretty large bullet in the days after the crash.

Ironically, even Leo's worst trade made him a million bucks. Not all traders are that lucky. Oftentimes, a trader's worst trade ends his trading career, but Leo Melamed has lived something of a charmed life.

The Worst of Times

I n 1978 silver was trading for roughly $5 an ounce. The price of all precious metals had increased dramatically since the early 1970s, when then-President Richard Nixon took the United States off the gold standard, allowing gold prices to fluctuate and the dollar's value to float freely for the first time in the postwar world. It was one of the first events that would lead to brutal bouts of inflation the United States would suffer over the coming decade.

When the gold window closed that fateful day, inflation shocks rocked the United States. Wage and price spirals forced the imposition of wage and price freezes. And the 1973 Arab oil embargo only made matters worse, as gasoline prices exacerbated the pressures that began to eat away at the high standard of living most Americans enjoyed for the previous twenty-five years.

For the rest of the "me decade," various administrations attempted to halt the persistent crumbling of consumers' purchasing power. Gerald Ford's ill-fated effort to "Whip Inflation Now" (you remember WIN buttons, don't you?) had little impact on the problems of the day. Jimmy Carter's inept monetary policy maneuvers and infamous "malaise" speech did little to stir the economy out of its doldrums. In fact, by the late 1970s, the United States was caught in a seemingly inescapable quagmire of recession and inflation, an unusual mix of economic realities that ravaged everyone from Wall Street to Main Street.

The only beneficiaries of that uniquely difficult time were the owners of hard assets. Their values increased constantly as inflation eroded the purchasing power of financial investments like stocks and bonds. As inflation grew worse, oil prices, real estate prices, and the prices for silver and gold began to rally creating opportunities. In that environment Leo Melamed made his worst trade over, but he also made his first million.

Traders' Tales

In 1978, as the economy lurched from growth to recession, badgered by rising prices, Melamed and his partner knew a good deal when they saw it. That good deal that they spotted was silver selling at $5 an ounce. As inflationary pressures continued to mount, Leo and his investing partner reasoned that precious metals would become an attractive investment. Unlike financial assets, metals increase in value during inflationary times, maintaining their purchasing power and providing investors with a hedge against the rising prices of goods and services.

So Leo and his partner began accumulating a large position in silver futures on New York's Commodity Exchange. By autumn of the following year, Leo and his partner had purchased two hundred silver futures contracts each. In those days, one silver futures contract represented the right to purchase 10,000 ounces of silver at a given price by a certain future date. In short, Leo Melamed controlled two million ounces of silver through his futures holdings, which he'd bought between about $5 and $8 an ounce. His partner controlled another two million ounces.

In the world of futures trading, the owner of silver futures need not actually buy the silver outright and store the metal in his office or at home. Owning the contracts means one has the right to purchase the silver at a set price by a future date. If one wants to maintain the holdings without ever exercising the option to take delivery of the real metals, one can simply roll over futures contracts from month to month, retaining control of the entire position until it is sold or delivery of the physical commodity is taken.

Leo did neither by October of 1979. He just kept rolling his silver holdings over, watching the price of poor man's gold run from $5 to $9.50 an ounce in a little more than a year. In a year's time his investment had nearly doubled.

By now, both Leo and his partner had gotten a tad nervous about the gargantuan trade they had undertaken. Big commodity trading firms had taken much bigger positions in the past and would in the future, but for Leo and Co., this was the biggest speculation they'd ever made, so nervousness was not an unjustified emotion.

With the price of silver having nearly doubled, Leo began to think about taking his profits and walking away from the trade. A "double" in a trader's world is a gift from God and should usually be taken with much thanks and great humility. With that gift given him, Leo consulted with a friend from Philipp Brothers, the renowned commodity trading house of the time, to find out what he should do with this trade. His friend counseled him to be cautious. While he never recommended that Leo and his partner sell out, the Philipp's expert suggested that silver had most likely seen its best days and that it might be prudent to take the double and run. In the final analysis, the Philipp's chap thought silver could go a bit higher than anyone expected, as markets are wont to do, but he told Leo that in this bull run, silver had probably already enjoyed the bulk of this move.

Leo huddled with his partner to discuss strategy. The silver market's impressive run had stalled, as their Philipp's friend said it might, but Leo and his partner weren't entirely sure the bull market was, in fact, over for good. So they decided to hold their position for one more week. If by the end of another week, the shiny metal failed to resume its uptrend they would dump their entire position and take their profits.

That's what they did. And in 1979 Leo Melamed made his first million dollars. A great trade for two young turks who took a flier on a chancey commodity and scored big. But to Leo today, this trade is among the worst he ever made. For in less than thirty days from when they dumped four million ounces of silver at about $9 an ounce, the world learned of the Hunt brothers' efforts to corner the silver market.

The Hunt brothers, a trio of Texas billionaires, staged a coup in the silver market as the 1970s wound to a close. They tried to buy up all the silver in the world, all the time driving up its price and, in the end, profiting greatly from the ploy.

As word leaked out of the dwindling supplies of silver, the price of the semiprecious metal began to surge, jumping higher, inexorably higher, day after day after day.

At the New York Commodity Exchange, silver soared to the allowable daily price limit repeatedly—until it reached $35 an ounce! That was three and a half times the price for which Leo Melamed sold his two million ounces of silver. Leo recalls that silver "rested" at $35 an ounce for a short time, and then launched a final assault to $50, where it finally peaked out.

The attempted corner in the silver market failed. The Hunt brothers eventually saw the empire collapse as their precious metals scam faltered and their oil businesses ultimately went bust. But in a short time, their efforts at market manipulation drove silver from $5 an ounce to $50. It was a trading opportunity that Leo Melamed missed, even though his hunch about the silver market turned out to be right.

Leo says he never bothered to calculate the exact amount he might have made had he stayed in the market just a little longer, but he knows he left millions of dollars on the table. Even so, he also knows his worst trade ever made him a million bucks. Not bad for a lousy trade.

The Best of Times

By 1987 Leo Melamed was chairman of the Chicago Mercantile Exchange, the place where stock and currency futures change hands. The most popular futures contract at the "Merc" is the Standard & Poor's 500 contract, which is based on the Standard & Poor's 500 stock index. The S&P 500 is a basket of stocks representing five hundred of the nation's biggest and most important industrial and service companies. It's a blue-chip index, but it is far more representative of the broad market's health than, say, the Dow Jones industrial average, which houses only thirty individual equities.

Large institutional investors often buy the S&P 500 to take advantage of the diverse nature of the stocks in the average and the deep liquidity (tradability) of the stocks that make up the basket. Because the underlying average was so popular among institutional investors, innovators in the market, like Leo Melamed, created a futures contract on the S&P 500, allowing investors to hedge their exposure to stocks by buying or selling futures contracts against their stock market positions.

Ironically, the development of futures for stocks gave rise to some very complicated trading strategies that gave savvy investors the opportunity to profit from the inherent price discrepancies between an actual basket of stocks and the associated futures contracts. These strategies, known as "program trading" and "portfolio insurance" would one day cause great volatility in the financial markets and would be blamed, at least partly, for precipitating the 1987 stock market crash.

Leo Melamed never agreed with those who said stock index futures increased the volatility. He said futures helped liquidity in the marketplace and allowed investors an opportunity to hedge their exposure to stocks, not just to speculate aimlessly. It is an arcane Wall Street argument to be sure, but one that would play heavily in discussions surrounding the October Massacre of 1987.

As the program trading debate grew more heated in the early days of 1986, some financial physicists at an outfit called Leland, O'Brien, and Rubenstein (LOR) created an investment strategy that would come to be called portfolio insurance. The "rocket scientists" at LOR devised mathematical models that showed how one could protect a stock portfolio from an inevitable downturn in stocks. They reasoned that if a money manager sold a corresponding number of stock index futures short when the market suffered a serious setback, the profit from the short sale of futures would offset the decline in the underlying basket of stocks. It was a simple concept that told money managers to sell a corresponding amount of futures short against their portfolios and to continue to do so every time the market dropped 7%.

Sounded good on paper, but no one ever stopped to wonder what would happen if all money managers employed the same strategy on the same day at the same time. They found out the answer to that question on October 19, 1987. The Dow Jones industrial average fell 22% in a single day—a whopping 508 points. It was the biggest crash in the history of the stock market and futures would take part of the blame for the calamity. In that environment Leo Melamed, the chairman of the nation's largest stock futures exchange, would make his best trade.

Throughout 1987 Leo Melamed was growing increasingly nervous about the state of the stock market. It had been years since stocks suffered a true bear market (a decline of 20% or more). Since 1982, stock prices more or less moved regularly to new all-time highs, stopping to digest the gains in 1984 and 1985, and then rocketing forward in 1986 and 1987. To be sure, it was not always a smooth run for the roses. The advent of program trading and other arcane options and futures-related strategies caused wild swings in the market, the likes of which had not been seen since the heady days of the Roaring Twenties. In fact, the near stratospheric rise of stock prices and the renewed volatility caused seasoned market veterans to draw inevitable comparisons to the days that lead up to Black Tuesday in 1929.

Beginning in January 1987, the stock market began to vault even higher in earnest. By August 25, the Dow had jumped nearly 1,000 points for the year, peaking at 2722. By most historical measures, stock prices were expensive. Classic valuation measures suggested that stock prices had not been as overvalued, or as dangerously high, since 1929! By September of 1987 a host of factors began to make stocks look increasingly less attractive than they had been only months earlier.

Leo Melamed recognized the signs of an impending top in stock prices. He began to play the market from the "short side," selling stock and stock index futures, in anticipation of a big decline in prices. If he was right, he would sell stocks at the top and then buy them back cheaper later on. Leo used the futures contracts that he devised to speculate on the market's decline.

In the five days leading up to the crash, Leo made a hefty profit by shorting the S&P 500. He remembers closing out his short position on Friday, October 16, the day the Dow plummeted 108 points. That week the Dow had dropped about 350 points, the worst week in market history. Leo made a lot of money, but more importantly, he salvaged his career by not being short on the following day. On Monday, October 19, the market came unglued. Portfolio insurance, that wild, futures-oriented strategy helped to ensure a market decline of epic proportions.

Today Leo knows he could have made an enormous killing had he shorted the market for just one more day. But the futures he helped to create were quickly blamed for the market debacle. Had he profited directly from this misery, he would have ended up a scurrilous figure in market history.

Right or wrong, futures were vilified in the press for their role in the '87 crash. Leo Melamed—a central figure in their development—feels lucky not to have benefited from the decline that fateful day. Leo learned that some of the best trades ever are the trades not made.

The Trading Desk

Picture a room half the size of a football field, lined with desks, computers, and phones. Visualize hundreds of people manning those desks, computers, and phones and all talking, yelling, or screaming at the same time. Or even better, picture a large talkative family at the dinner table, multiply that by a hundred and you've got it. That's what a Wall Street trading desk looks and sounds like nearly every day of the year. At the desk, brokers and traders buy and sell stocks, bonds, or commodities on behalf of their clients or their firms. It is a gigantic, high-tech pressure-cooker where millions of dollars can be made or lost every session. Phone lights blink constantly, computer screens flash quotes, green or red, bright or dark. The trading desk is host to a cacophony of finance, a maddening din that takes its toll on even the most seasoned professional.

Many Wall Street traders work in that environment. In that dense, trying atmosphere, the haggard and frenzied players often need to blow off a little steam. Sometimes their pranks are witty and harmless, sometimes they are downright crude. Still other times the practical jokes, bleeps, and blunders are virtually unrepeatable.

The trading desk, by the way, is the place where all jokes told in this country originate. Traders of Wall Street are trained to process information so quickly that it doesn't just end with the buying and selling of securities. In any situation, comic or tragic, they are quite capable of finding the irony. Whether it was the tragic explosion of the space shuttle *Challenger*, the stock market crash of 1987, or even the O. J. Simpson trial, traders generally find the humor in everything.

Perhaps it is because of the pressure of their situation. Every day, for 390 grueling minutes, 23,400 pressure-packed seconds, traders are on the hook for millions of dollars in profits or losses. The intensity of their profession forces them to respond to any event in rather hair-trigger fashion, even when it is not very fashionable to do so.

Strung Out

The trading desk can be a pressure-packed place to work. Whirring computer screens, ringing phones, lines lighting up, the hollering, screaming, and shouting can all be quite a lot to handle five days a week, fifty-two weeks a year. The pace on Wall Street is either maddeningly quick or mind-numbingly slow. Very few days are in-between.

The development of modern technology has quickened the pace of trading activity in the financial markets to quantum speed. Wall Street today is markedly different from twenty-five years ago, before the advent of digital technology and computers.

Joe Spendly, a veteran of nearly thirty years on the Street recalls "the old days"—before computers made trading rooms such a mad, mad, mad world. Spendly enjoys the fruits of his labors in the markets. He loves to dine in Manhattan, attend the theatre, and listen to opera at the Met—a culture vulture from Wall Street if there ever was one. He is a veteran of many campaigns, working at large New York commodity houses and major Manhattan trust banks. He's held a variety of jobs from trading currencies to handling customer accounts. He's seen trading activities take their toll on countless players who couldn't make the grade.

Woody Allen told a joke of how his father became "technologically unemployed." Woody described how his father was replaced at his job by a tiny electronic device that does his father's work. Only it does it better and faster. The depressing thing, Woody went on, is that his mother went out and bought one.

Joe Spendly tells a similar story about a fellow named George.

George was a quiet sort who worked with Joe at a trust bank in New York, back in the early 1970s. Trust banks manage money and engage in a host of client-driven businesses for well-heeled investors who need customized financial services. Trust banks also frequently trade securities, both for the house account and for clients. George was a clerk who was charged with some of the more menial duties at the trading desk: answering phones.

Back in the early 1970s, however, trading rooms were not nearly as complex as they are today. They were sophisticated for their time, to be sure, but nothing like they are now.

Spendly remembers the installation of a new phone system at his octagonal trading desk. The new system had thirty or forty lines. It was laid into the oversized trading desk, making the entire console blink and ring with every new call coming in.

STRUNG OUT

George never mastered Wall Street's high-tech game. He was always being yelled at.

"George, grab the phone."

"Line one, George."

"Phone's ringing, George."

"George, get the goddamn phone!"

Finally one day George just snapped. After a host of commands to "get the phone," George went berserk and began jumping up on top of the trading desk. He pulled off his shoes and socks and started pressing the phone's buttons simultaneously with his hands and feet. He wasn't joking around.

Spendly remembers calling the bank's in-house medical team, telling them, "one of our boys is a little ill."

The team arrived and took George away. Joe never saw him again.

Political Banter

Bobby Antolini is a big trader on Wall Street. In his many years trading over-the-counter (OTC) stocks (what we now call NASDAQ), he's had some wild times. Bobby is a big man on the Street—both in size and stature. He's traded everywhere. He's made money. He's made friends, and maybe even a few enemies. Today, he remains a well-respected OTC trader, heading the desk at Donaldson, Lufkin, and Jenrette—a firm started by, you guessed it, three men, named Donaldson, Lufkin, and Jenrette. The most notable of the three, William Donaldson, retired in 1994 as chairman of the New York Stock Exchange.

Back in the wilder days of Wall Street, when smaller firms made markets in smaller stocks, Bobby Antolini was a major trader at Unterberg, Towbin. Tommy Unterberg and Bob Towbin were, and still are, master players in the OTC game. They underwrote the small stocks for little companies that needed capital. Bobby Antolini traded them on the OTC market, buying and selling small stocks for his institutional clients and his firm. He was also a major prankster and a Wall Street character whose mind is as fast as his order execution.

Like most players on the trading desk, Bobby Antolini never heard a flippant remark he didn't repeat. Sometimes, a wry comment is just what the desk needs to brighten the moment. Other times, some of the banter on the Street can come dangerously close to grounds for dismissal. In a single line Antolini nearly accomplished both. But everyone who heard him said it was worth it.

Bobby's boss, Bob Towbin was a muckety-muck in Democratic Party circles in the 1970s and early 1980s. He had a cadre of friends from Congress and throughout the nation's capital. Most important to him, though, was one of the Kennedy clan. Ted Kennedy and Bob Towbin were friends. Every Washingtonian needs a Wall Street money man.

One day in the early 1980s, Towbin was giving the Massachusetts Senator a tour of the trading floor. Everyone knows this senator has had his share of difficulties over the last many years, not just from the loss of three brothers, but from his involvement in the Chappaquiddick episode.

As you probably recall, Kennedy was driving home late one night after a rollicking good time with his woman friend, Mary Jo Kopechne, when he drove off a bridge into the "dark and murky" waters surrounding Chappaquiddick Island. Kennedy left to get help and Kopechne drowned. The incident caused a scandal that dominated the headlines for months and most likely prevented the fourth Kennedy son from ever making a serious run at the White House.

A few years after Chappaquiddick, Kennedy visited the trading floor at Unterberg, Towbin. First Towbin spoke to his traders and then asked the Senator to say a few words and mingle with the group. After they finished and Towbin was ushering his good friend to the exit, Bobby Antolini asked the group, "Hey girls, the Senator's leaving. Anyone need a ride home?"

PIMCO's Swinging Dick

Most of the antics in the financial community are certainly harmless enough. There's a lot of kid stuff that goes on but most of the office pranks are like gags anywhere else: harmless, mindless, but usually funny at the time.

The prank you're about to read about, though, is probably the biggest, baddest practical joke ever played on a client. If this client, Bill Gross, were to have been described in Michael Lewis's *Liar's Poker*, *he* would have been the "biggest swinging dick" in the book. But Bill never worked at Salomon Brothers, which is the ground zero in *Liar's Poker*. Instead, he's been building PIMCO into a money-management powerhouse over the last twenty-odd years. His success was almost derailed, though, by a prank that makes other Wall Street practical jokes look saintly in comparison.

Bill Gross is the biggest bond fund manager in the country. As the head of the Pacific Investment Management Company (PIMCO), Bill runs $65 billion dollars of other people's money. With that much money in tow, Gross is a major client of nearly all of the Wall Street firms.

As a bond fund manager, Bill Gross buys bonds. All kinds of bonds. Treasury bonds, mortgage bonds, foreign bonds, corporate bonds, junk bonds, Mexican "Brady" bonds. If it's a bond, Bill buys it. Unless, of course, he happens not to like the bond market. Then he just buys Treasury bills, for safekeeping.

He is an astute investor and former marathon runner, whose quiet patient manner belies his reputation as one of the most shrewd buyers and traders of bonds in the country, if not the world. But one purchase that he presumably made nearly got him into big trouble with the folks who regulate the securities markets. Big trouble.

Back in 1991, Salomon Brothers, the venerable Wall Street trading house and investment bank, was embroiled in a bond trading scandal that nearly toppled the old-line firm. At the center of the scandal was one trader's desire to corner the market in several different Treasury securities, potentially earning the firm a large profit and himself a large bonus.

The trader in question, Paul Mozer, was ultimately dismissed and penalized. His superiors, John Merriweather and Salomon's chairman, John Guttfreund, also ended up leaving the firm as a result of their employee's misdeeds. Salomon was fined and nearly closed down by the regulators, until its largest investor, the famed "Oracle of Omaha," Warren Buffett, rode to the rescue and cleaned house.

The original scam involved billions of dollars of falsified bids for U.S. government bonds that Mozer submitted on behalf of unsuspecting clients. By using customer accounts, Mozer could buy more bonds than Salomon was allowed to buy directly from the government. His cornering the market in several different Treasury notes pushed up their prices, artificially inflating the value of Salomon's bond inventories. It almost worked. But, the hue and cry from other trading houses was so loud, as they were forced to pay ever-increasing prices for certain securities, that Mozer got caught.

Here's where Bill Gross comes in.

Paul Mozer and some other Salomon traders wanted to play a practical joke on a retiring saleswoman who had never done a billion dollar deal. She, herself, reported to a boss everyone called "Billion dollar Bill," so named for his propensity to buy and sell huge blocks of bonds at any given moment.

Well, Mozer wanted this saleswoman to know what a billion dollar deal felt like before she left the firm. So, he arranged to have PIMCO submit a bogus $1 billion bid to the retiring saleswoman, the day she was departing the firm. The bid, Mozer promised, would be canceled at his desk and PIMCO would never be required to take delivery of the bond.

As part of the joke, PIMCO would be told the retiring saleswoman botched the job and she would subsequently be "blamed" for failing to handle her most lucrative trade. Sounded funny at the time, they say.

Sure enough, a clerk misread Mozer's instructions and actually submitted the bid for $1 billion dollars worth of thirty-year Treasury bonds. Because bonds sold by the government are allotted on a prorate basis among the bidders who want them, PIMCO was awarded $870 million worth of bonds without ever knowing it. The Salomon trader called Bill Gross and apologized profusely for the error. He would not have to pay for the bonds.

To complicate matters further, the Salomon trader transferred the bonds to another customer account, failing to tell *that* customer that it was the proud new owner of $870 million in bonds either. The whole episode led to a great deal of embarrassment for everyone involved. The "joke" happened just as Salomon was being investigated for submitting a host of false bids for bonds in an effort to corner the market.

Bill Gross was summoned to the offices of the Securities and Exchange Commission. He had to explain that his billion dollar bid for bonds was nothing more than a practical joke. Lucky for Bill, the SEC had a sense of humor.

Take Another Tick

The major brokerage houses on Wall Street trade in a wide variety of securities. Big houses like Merrill Lynch, Goldman Sachs, Bear Stearns, or Prudential have rather large, elaborate desks, where stocks, bonds, currencies, and commodities are all bought and sold. Some of the buying is for clients—large institutional clients in some cases, mom-and-pop investors in others. And, of course, the house can trade for its own account as well. All this activity makes for a rather vibrant atmosphere inside the walls of Wall Street.

The stock desks of major brokerage houses are principally located in New York's financial district, but the bond desks can be in Chicago, the home of the famous futures exchanges, where not only commodities but bond futures are also traded.

Bond futures are commodity-like instruments that allow investors to buy a derivative contract based on bonds. Usually these are Treasury bonds, Uncle Sam's debt paper. Bond futures do not pay interest, though, like regular bonds. Instead, the price of a bond futures contract rises and falls with the gains and losses scored in the underlying cash bond itself. An investor who wants to control a large chunk of bonds can do so far more cheaply by buying bond futures because the investor has only to put up a small margin (or downpayment) to buy quite a large supply of Treasury bonds.

The U.S. bond market is one of the largest securities markets in the world, regardless of how it is priced. On any given day, billions and billions of dollars worth of bonds change hands in the bond market. Because Uncle Sam has been running such large budget deficits in the last many years, there are hundreds of billions of dollars worth of bonds, even trillions, sloshing around the financial world. And Wall Streeters trade in that market quite aggressively as we soon will see.

Now the bond market has some quirky characteristics you may need to know about. Individual investors who buy bonds usually do so to capture the interest payments that Uncle Sam makes when he borrows money. They buy bonds for safety and income since the government has never welched on a debt yet. So individual investors fork over their hard-earned dough to capture the ample but safe interest payment that U.S. bonds offer. In three months to thirty years, whatever the denomination of the bond, the investor's principal will be returned, perfectly safe, no more strings attached.

However, big traders on Wall Street rarely buy a bond for the interest payment. They buy bonds when they think interest rates will fall. (Bond prices go up as interest rates fall, since the value of existing interest income goes up, as new bonds are issued with lower rates of interest.) They then hope to resell the bonds later for a capital gain. If they have to wait a while for prices to go up, they are compensated for waiting, since they'll take whatever interest payments are made in the interim.

Really big traders take the whole process a step further. They buy bond futures when they expect interest rates to fall. Bond futures are like commodity contracts: They allow traders to speculate in the bond market without necessarily ever owning the bonds themselves. Traders can use borrowed money to buy bond futures and sell out of their positions if they score a profit. They magnify their gains using leverage, because the Chicago Board of Trade requires big futures traders to put down a small sum to purchase their bond futures. So with a little capital, they can control a lot of bond futures contracts and score big if they bet right.

Hopefully you're getting the sense that betting on bond futures can be a big money game where every little move in bond prices can mean a lot to a highly leveraged buyer.

Bonds themselves are traded in a rather odd way. They are priced in 32nds of a dollar. In Street parlance 32nds are known as ticks. That fact leads us to a story about how big trades at the big bond desks rely quite heavily on clear communication, especially when so many words rhyme with tick.

A Chicago bond expert tells a tale of a young clerk at Prudential Securities' office in the Windy City. The clerk was on the phone with a major client who played heavily in the bond market and speculated quite heavily in bond futures. It was not unusual for this client to buy several thousand bond contracts in a given trade. That type of activity can prove quite expensive and quite risky if the bond market happens to be unusually volatile or if the market should make an unexpected U-turn. Be that as it may, the client is on the phone with a Prudential clerk, a well-meaning novice who is taking one of the biggest orders he's ever seen.

The client asks to buy the bond at a price of 98 and 8/32 in an unusually brisk market where prices are changing by the second. The young clerk nervously attempted to fill the big customer's order, anxious to please the client.

"I can fill your order at 98 and 8/32 bid. The bond is offered at 98 and 9."

As he begins the process of filling the request, the price of the bond begins to rally.

The clerk apologetically informs his client that since talking the bond moved up in price, by a tick. "The bond is bid at 98 and 9."

To which the customer says, "OK, buy it at 9."

"Too late, it's bid at 10."

"OK, take a thousand at 10."

"Well, it's 10 bid, 11 asked."

By this point, the customer is getting a little "ticked" himself. Each tick in a bond contract costs $31.25. On a thousand bond contracts, every increase of one tick costs the buyer $31,250. A few more ticks and the extra cost is in the six figures.

The client says, "All right, pay 11."

The clerk: "It's 11 bid, 12 traded."

The customer is incensed!

"Aw, you're a dick!"

"Take another tick? OK, you're filled at 12."

The customer says, "I didn't say, 'take a tick,' you idiot, I said, 'you're a dick!' "

The kid says, "I might be a dick, but you're filled at 12 on a thousand!" The client paid an extra $125,000 for his thousand contracts. Lucky for the kid, the client made money.

Ticker Symbols

A human heart is often referred to as "a ticker." Like a clock, the rhythmic ticking of the heart keeps the beat in life. And like a clock, when the heart stops ticking, time's up! On Wall Street, there is a ticker as well. It is the pulse of the market. It carries on it the prices of individual stocks. And like a heart, if this ticker stops, something is clearly wrong.

The ticker on Wall Street today is an electronic one though not unlike the ones of days gone by. It still prints out the price and volume of active stocks, offering crucial information to all those who understand how to read the tape. In some ways, the ticker is like the electrocardiogram (EKG) of the stock market. And traders are, at least a little, like doctors. They read the tape every few minutes to determine the health of the market and they take preventative or remedial action, depending on what the ticker tells them.

But, like an EKG, a ticker can be difficult to read. To understand the ticker, one must be intimately familiar with ticker symbols, the three- or four-letter symbols that identify individual stocks in the stock market. Often, the symbols are easily recognizable acronyms for a company. IBM's ticker symbol is, not surprisingly, IBM. The Toys 'R' Us symbol is TOY.

On the New York and American Exchanges, symbols are one to three letters. On the NASDAQ stock market, company symbols contain four letters, allowing for more intriguing identities. Mr. Coffee's symbol is JAVA. Summit Technology, a maker of lasers used in eye surgery owns the symbol, BEAM. In the 1980s, the Mustang Ranch in Nevada actually went public, selling stock in the NASDAQ market. Think of the fun had by all coming up with a four-letter ticker symbol for a brothel! The symbol turned out to be quite mundane, but Wall Streeters had much fun fantasizing about the possibilities.

By now you get the picture. Ticker symbols appear on the ticker tape. And traders read the tape to get the pulse of the market. But what happens when the pulse of a trader gets confused with the pulse of the market? Harvey Eisen recalls the results were nearly tragic.

Harvey Eisen is among Wall Street's most respected money managers. These days he manages corporate money at Travellers, the big insurance and financial services concern that owns the Smith Barney brokerage.

Eisen has had a colorful career, as Wall Street pedigrees go. A University of Missouri grad, he began his days on the Street in the 1960s, when the so-called big gun money managers like Freddie Carr and Jerry Tsai ran "go-go" mutual funds. Those were heady days when mutual fund mania was at its height.

Eisen also spent some time at the now-defunct Drexel Burnham Lambert and Sun America before ending up at Travellers.

Like most money managers on Wall Street, he learned the game from the bottom up. While working at the trading desk Eisen learned ticker symbols like the back of his hand. He recalls a day when one colleague confused a critical message for help with a stock symbol.

During one frenetic day, several years back, Eisen recalls the crush of business was taking its toll on the trading desk. Traders were shouting out buy and sell orders, trying to match up their customers in an effort to do business.

"Who wants IBM at a quarter?" one trader shouted out.

"I got a half a million CAT (Caterpillar, Inc.) at a half," yelled another.

One of the traders working the desk began to feel a little queasy as the day wore on, feeling the pressure of the frantic pace. As his condition grew worse, his heart began to pound and his head grew light. Worried that he was in the midst of a heart attack, the troubled trader stood up from his chair and yelled, "Does anybody here know CPR?"

"Wait, don't do anything. I think I have a buyer!" was the only response from the desk. The traders were no help.

As it turned out, the victim did keel over and was rushed to the hospital by ambulance. But he was fine—just anxiety and indigestion. It was a good thing for him, too. The only three letters traders know are ticker symbols!

Women on Wall Street

For nearly all of its history, Wall Street has been a male bastion. New York's financial district has personified the old boys network, and it has only been since the 1970s that women have had any discernible presence whatsoever on the Street.

In today's Wall Street environment, most female financial professionals will tell you that it doesn't matter to their clients if an expert has green skin, blue eyes, and is from another planet, so long as he/she/it can deliver superior performance. But that has not always been the case.

Women were not wanted on Wall Street for quite a number of years. Those who chose to work in financial services bore numerous insults, worked longer and harder than a lot of their male peers, and were forced to put up with the locker room mentality.

One woman has successfully challenged the dominance of men in the most "manly" of arenas, the trading floor. Muriel Siebert, the Queen of Wall Street, was the first woman to ever own a seat on the floor of the New York Stock Exchange. From her perch on the floor, she would change the ways of the bastion of male-dominated capitalism, forever.

Muriel Siebert blazed the trail for a new breed of Wall Street women. After Muriel, women would not be confined to secretarial positions, back-office jobs, or support positions. And after Muriel would come the likes of Elaine Garzarelli, Abby Joseph Cohen, or Elizabeth Bramwell, women, who in their own right, would become among the most famous investors or analysts on the Street.

Although women have cracked the glass ceiling on the Street there are still very few women who have moved into the most elite ranks of the chief executive suite. With the exception of Siebert, who runs her own discount brokerage firm, there are no women who fill the top job at any of Wall Street's major brokerage houses.

No doubt, with time, that will change too. The women on Wall Street are a hearty lot who have the brains and the drive to make it to the top.

Here are some of their reminiscences of breaking into the ranks of the millionaires boy's club.

The Queen of Wall Street

Muriel Siebert is a college dropout with ten honorary degrees. Like so many successful people she has no sheepskin but doesn't lack an education. She was schooled at one of the best universities this country has to offer, the School of Hard Knocks. A degree from that college guarantees success, because the lessons learned there are far more practical and valuable than any theories taught in the ivory towers of academia.

Women on Wall Street

Mickey, as she is known to close friends and associates, is a gritty survivor. From rather humble beginnings she blazed a trail for other women of Wall Street. But Mickey did not arrive at her appointed place as the Queen of Wall Street without bearing some insult and some injury. Many times the old boys tried to keep her out of the network but they failed in their efforts. Muriel Siebert succeeded in the arena on Wall Street that was exclusively dominated by men—the rough and tumble trading floor.

Today she runs Muriel Siebert & Co., a discount brokerage firm she built from scratch. She is a scrappy woman, short, but powerfully built, with platinum blond hair and a slightly raspy voice. She is somewhat reminiscent of Lauren Bacall, with a slightly sultry appearance and assertive air that lets you know who's in charge of the room, once she walks in.

But Mickey wasn't always a member of Wall Street's royal family. In fact, she barely made her way into the lower crust of Wall Street when she first appeared on the scene, a fresh young face from Cleveland, Ohio.

Mickey Siebert's father died of cancer while she was still in college. He was a young man in his mid-50s, who Mickey tried to take care of as best she could. He fell victim not only to the disease but also to some experimental cancer operations attempted in the early 1950s. Because of her father's illness Mickey failed to finish college. She cut classes to see him and spent minimal efforts in her studies. When she actually did study, it was accounting. Those were the only classes Mickey found she could pass without actually attending. She had a natural feel for numbers, a skill she exercised not only in her ultimate field of endeav-

or, but also useful in another one of her passions, playing bridge.

Her lack of a formal education would slow her entrance to Wall Street. It would not, however, keep her from living the American dream.

Still, it was tough going for Mickey in the early days. She was refused a job at the United Nations because she spoke only one language. Her cousin, Alvin Roseman, was a U.S. ambassador to the UN but he couldn't provide her with what she needed for a life in the diplomatic corps—a college degree and a second language.

Wall Street was next. But its premier firm, Merrill Lynch, also turned Mickey down for want of a piece of paper. So she stopped the attempts at being diplomatic and lied. She told her next potential employer that she was a college graduate. And so Bache and Company hired her. (Bache has since been absorbed by Prudential Securities.) It was a lie she would maintain until she applied for her seat on the NYSE, when she demonstrated that a dropout with grit and guts could make it in the really big leagues of finance.

She began as an analyst in training for Bache in December of 1954. She spent her first six months learning to analyze the balance sheets of some pretty mundane businesses, like chemicals, railroads, buses, and trucking. But after those six months were up, and Muriel had paid her dues, she became a senior analyst who was given a considerable amount of responsibility but not a lot more money.

Still, Muriel was lucky enough to follow businesses that were up and coming and whose profits were very much dependent upon classic accounting considerations, an area in which she had some formal schooling. In fact, three of the nation's most exciting new businesses were quite tricky from an accounting perspective. The airline, movie, and TV industries had rather arcane methods of accounting. Muriel sensed opportunity in these fledgling businesses, so she made a name for herself by becoming an astute observer of the sexy industries of the mundane 1950s. She stayed at Bache for three years. Her beginning salary was $65 a week; it was $135 when she left.

After some early successes she moved from firm to firm, often underpaid because of her gender. When Muriel went to Shields & Company (not to be confused with the Shields & Co. on Wall Street today) the company paid her $9,000. That was with three years experience. By contrast, male trainees, fresh out of college, earned $8,500. Muriel changed jobs three times in her career because she didn't make what the men were making. It was one of the injustices that eventually prompted her to start her own firm.

She did however, get a series of lucky breaks, mostly from customers and clients for whom she made money. And on Wall Street, making money for your clients is the bottom line. If you can do that for them, they will do a lot for you. Once that's established, your gender ultimately becomes a nonissue. Muriel Siebert always made money for her clients.

Mickey learned a lot from the men on Wall Street. She learned how to use four-letter words from David Finkel, who ran Finkel, Seskus and Walsteder, a brokerage firm where she spent some time. Finkel used profane language the way Julia Child uses spices—quite liberally and with great panache.

He once asked Mickey if she had called Jerry Tsai to solicit business from the legendary money manager of the 1960s. She said, no, she didn't have anything to sell him.

Finkel's response was, quite simply, "I don't give a damn if you have anything to sell him or not. You call Jerry Tsai." Muriel called Jerry Tsai and learned very quickly how to use the language of the floor. It helped her fit in early.

Mickey was learning the ropes. She remembers the necessity of being able to hold her liquor just like the guys. A lot of business on the Street is done over dinner and drinks. There are none-too-few salespeople on Wall Street who have to be as good at stashing away alcohol as they are stashing away cash.

Mickey was once escorted home by some senior Lockheed executives after a business meeting. Upon departing the Plaza Hotel they stopped at the first bar on the right side of the street. Then they crossed the street and stopped at the first bar on the left. They zigzagged for ten blocks until Muriel arrived home. She zigzagged to bed after a tough night out with the boys. Years later, Muriel wrote a report about a failing Lockheed that was submitted to Congress, when the federal government was forced to bail the struggling aircraft maker out of a mess. Mickey's study of the company's potential failure and its impact on the entire airline industry helped influence Congress's decision to bail Lockheed out. It was a favor the company never forgot.

For Mickey Siebert this was all part and parcel of breaking in. In many ways she enjoyed it, though from her tone today you sense she wishes it would have been just a little easier to get started in this business.

Eventually she mastered the field and started her own firm. But it was her friend Jerry Tsai who encouraged Muriel to buy her own seat on the New York Stock Exchange. Tsai pointed out that there were no laws banning women from the Big Board floor and that she could do herself a great service if she took that important step forward in her career. So in 1967 she did just that.

But not all the men on Wall Street proved quite so friendly. Executives at the Big Board were happy to sell Muriel a seat, as long as a bank provided a letter of credit. It seemed simple, but there was a catch, a catch-22-style catch. The major banks she approached for the funds said they'd provide a letter of credit if she could get the seat at the Exchange.

It was the same predicament that many trailblazers faced. The help offered was really no help at all. The offers were just transparent schemes to prevent Mickey, a woman, from entering an all-male bastion. But, like many other pioneers, she would not be denied.

Fortunately for Muriel, a male friend at the Chase Bank provided the letter and the loan, a silent partner, so to speak, in the suffrage movement that was just beginning on Wall Street. For $445,000 ($150,000 of which was Mickey's own cash) Muriel Siebert became the first woman ever to buy a seat on the New York Stock Exchange. For the next ten years, she and 1,365 men would work the floor of the exchange. She would be the only woman until Jane Larkin, a partner at Hirsch & Co., became a member. Unlike Mickey, Jane lasted only three months.

Inside Chase, the loan officer, ironically, was among those making bets that he'd never have the opportunity to lend Mickey the money. He thought it would be a cold day in hell before the Exchange ever sold a seat to a woman. He was wrong.

To be sure he got paid back, the Chase executive gave Mickey her first few orders. The orders were big enough to ensure that Mickey's commissions equaled the exact amount she owed the bank for her first month's payment. The commissions generated by the orders equaled the loan payment down to the penny. Mickey Siebert was in business.

Muriel made history on the Exchange floor, walking across those ancient wooden slats in her alligator shoes, executing the first floor trade by a woman in the history of the U.S. markets.

Over time, Mickey forced other concessions in the all-male world of Wall Street. The New York Stock Exchange had to put in a ladies room to accommodate Mickey. It was forced to change the rules banning women from the lunch-rooms, the lounges, and the game room. The changes were made—reluctantly. But today, because of Muriel Siebert, the Queen of Wall Street, and even the Queen of England, can dine at the Exchange's table.

"Honey, You Can Get Right to It"

Life in the markets can be a bit tough on women. It's not just the salty humor, or the sophomoric behavior—women simply have to work much harder than men to be accepted into the oldest of old boy networks. Up until the last fifteen years, in fact, women were relegated to support positions in brokerage houses and trading companies. They did secretarial work or back-office paperwork. Very few women rose to prominence on Wall Street before the "Roaring Eighties." Women were toiling diligently back in the 1970s paying their dues, and sometimes, dealing with men who weren't quite ready to have a woman help them with their finances.

Cathy Jones is one such woman. She's an economist who tracks the bond market for Prudential Securities. Her office is in downtown Chicago, a downright wild place where the trading desk can get particularly raunchy and pugnacious. But Cathy has taken it all in stride. She's a smart woman, and smart looking, with slightly oversized glasses, an appearance that belies a much more irreverent personality than you'd expect from a woman who crunches numbers for a living. She is quite quick with a joke and has some unusually keen insights on life.

Cathy Jones began her career as an agricultural economist, a proper start for a product of the heartland. She began counting beans, corn, pigs, and cattle in the 1970s, when the commodity markets were a particularly hot, well, commodity in the investment world. The 1970s, as you'll recall, were all about inflation. And no markets fare better than commodities when inflation is in full force. In short, Cathy entered her business at the right place and right time.

In her early days at PaineWebber, Cathy evaluated the prospects for the nation's agricultural markets, analyzing the impact of many factors on the supply of, and demand for, everything from pigs and hogs to corn and oats, offering her assessments to commodity traders and speculators. It was not an overly exciting position, but it was a solid first step in the business of market analysis.

The commodity markets can be volatile places where prices of goods rise and fall with frightening speed, creating and destroying fortunes as quickly as lightning strikes the plains. Commodity traders are a colorful lot, hair-trigger types, whose minds must be nimble in the fast-trading atmosphere of the Chicago futures pits. One of Cathy's favorite stories involves a morning conference call that she allowed her mother to attend, shortly after she began her career on LaSalle Street.

One of the firm's analysts was describing a particularly strong day in the pork belly market. Pork bellies are heavily traded commodities in Chicago. The bellies themselves are used to make bacon, so around Memorial Day, when BLT season starts, pork belly prices can move particularly fast as grocers across the country stock up in preparation for the summer season. During those seasonal frenzies prices tend to jump quickly as demand for the goods rises.

Cathy was waiting her turn to address the sales force to offer her assessments of the various markets she covered. But first, one of the firm's most colorful characters was queried on the state of the belly market.

"Bob! Bob, when's this market going to stop?"

Bob responded, "This market's like a honeymoon hard-on. It just won't come down."

Tough act to follow. Cathy's mom was gracious enough to never discuss that incident with Cathy, even though she must have harbored not just a few concerns about her daughter's chosen profession.

Shortly after that embarrassing moment, Cathy Jones embarked on her first business trip ever as a young, female professional. It was another experience that would cause her to blush, just a bit.

Cathy's first business trip came shortly after PaineWebber acquired a small, regional brokerage house that catered to accounts in the Midwest. After acquiring the little house on the prairie, PaineWebber moved quickly to secure the firm's clients. So PaineWebber dispatched a group from the Chicago office on a three-city tour of the newly acquired firm's Nebraska offices. Cathy was among the lucky few chosen to head to Nebraska in mid December. (None of PaineWebber's more senior New York staff was interested in the trip, a surprise to no one in Chicago.)

The three-city tour took Cathy Jones and several other unfortunate souls to Lincoln, Grand Island, and Minden, Nebraska. These are three great places to go if you want to assess the quality of the winter wheat crop, but beyond that, this was hardly Jones's idea of a big business trip or a good time, for that matter.

Be that as it may, off she went to convince the local brokers and their clients that PaineWebber's research staff would be an invaluable asset to them. This was Cathy's big chance to do good. She traveled from town to town, winding up in Minden, Nebraska, on a Friday night in mid December of 1979. A Friday that was also her birthday. A Friday that also dumped mounds of snow onto the ground as a nasty blizzard kicked up. Cathy was cold and alone in a snowbound hamlet in Nebraska. Her colleagues had long-since departed, leaving the twenty-six-year-old agronomist on her own to guide the local brokers through the forecasting field. A little like the Wizard of Oz's Dorothy, she had a sneaking suspicion she wasn't in Kansas, anymore.

That night she was late for her first steak-fry with the local brokers. The bruising snowstorm that pelted the town held Cathy up for her date with destiny. Rushing into a local hotel, she ran to the front desk to inquire where the meeting was being held. She was directed to the Lincoln Room, where she quickly sprinted, all the while, refining her crop forecast in her head. By the time she stamped the snow from her boots she was fully prepared to greet the crowd and offer them some keen investing insights they would find invaluable for their next trades.

At the door, she was greeted by "Hank," who hurried her into the room, taking her coat, scarf, and hat.

"Oh, boy, I'm glad you're here," Hank said as he perused her business suit, which she wore with a tie.

Cathy apologized for her tardiness and jumped to the front of the room. The group of men, led by Hank, looked on with eager anticipation, hanging on Cathy's every word and subtle gesturing. Cathy began her forecast with a prediction on the size of the coming hog slaughter expected to take place in Chicago's meat markets in the near future.

The men in the room sat stone-faced, in rapt silence, clinging to Cathy's every word.

Finally, Hank rushed up to Cathy at the podium, looking a bit puzzled and disappointed. He exhorted her to proceed more quickly with her presentation.

"AREN'T YOU THE STRIPPER"

"Honey, why don't you just get right to it," he asked, implying she drop the coy act she had adopted to tease her audience.

"What are you talking about?" Cathy asked, somewhat incredulously.

"Aren't you the stripper?"

Hank was clearly confused but he managed to explain that it was his bachelor party and he wasn't much interested in charades—just skin.

Oops! Wrong room. The brokers were still waiting in the Washington room for their agricultural forecast. Cathy was only off by fifteen presidents.

To this day, she doesn't know if Hank ever got the presentation he was hoping for that Friday night.

Abby Road

Abby Joseph Cohen holds one of the most prestigious jobs on Wall Street. She is the cochair of the investment policy committee at Goldman Sachs & Co., one of Wall Street's oldest and most revered firms. Along with Steven Einhorn, Abby Cohen decides when Goldman's big clients should be in or out of the stock market, what percentage of bonds they should hold in their portfolios, or how many dollars they should invest in commodities. Like Muriel Siebert or Elaine Garzarelli, Abby Joseph Cohen is one of the few women to shatter the glass ceiling on Wall Street.

But she didn't shatter the glass without getting nicked by a few falling shards herself. After a stellar performance over the years, Abby doesn't feel the weight of discrimination any longer. She is among the few market strategists who have been blessed with an extraordinary gift for calling the twists and turns of the financial markets.

Twice in the last ten years she has been quite bullish on stocks when it was extraordinarily unpopular to be so. After the 1987 crash and again at the stock market lows of October 1990. But she learned very early in her career that it is much harder to be a woman in a field of men, than a raging bull in a clan of bears.

Cohen earned some very impressive educational credentials as a young woman preparing for a career. She was trained in both computer sciences and economics in her college days, a rare but valuable combination of skills for anyone entering the labor force in the early 1970s. She landed her first job at the Federal Reserve in Washington D.C., where she worked as an economist. After a stint in the public sector, she went private, taking a forecasting job at T. Rowe Price, the Baltimore-based mutual fund company. From there, it was on to Drexel Burnham Lambert and, finally, Goldman Sachs. She climbed quickly to the top on Wall Street, securing her position at Goldman in 1990. In only 15 years or so Abby moved into a coveted position that was at one time reserved only for men, at a firm that has a long tradition of being among the most exclusive investment clubs on Wall Street. But in her earliest days in the financial arena, the boys occasionally tried to get the best of her.

Abby Cohen was the quantitative analyst at T. Rowe Price. A quant, as the job is informally called on the Street, crunches a lot of rather arcane numbers to determine the direction of stock prices or the economy. Quants use indicators like interest rates, price/earnings ratios, and dividend yields to figure out whether stocks are cheap or dear, or whether the economy is strong or weak. From there, they make their investment recommendations accordingly.

Abby recalls coming to Manhattan to present her views on the economy and stock market to T. Rowe Price clients at the University Club. The elite, upscale fraternity was a second home to many of Wall Street's moneyed men, as are the Harvard Club and other such organizations that dot the tonier sections of Manhattan. Women were rarely, if ever, allowed into the plush, oak-paneled rooms of the

University Club, rooms that provided an after work haven for the upper crust. It was a barrier Abby Cohen was determined to break.

The information-hungry investors didn't care if the person doling out money-making information was man, woman, or Martian. But the administrators of the club certainly did. In fact, upon arriving at the University Club, Abby remembers the doorman telling her she could not enter.

"You can't come in," the uniformed guard informed her at the door.

"Why not?" she asked.

"Because you are a woman," was his response.

"Watch me," Abby challenged. With that, she walked in past the guard who yelled after her, threatening to call security.

Abby ignored the slight and headed in to do her job.

In 1995 Abby went back to the club to give another presentation for some "lovely, important people." It was her first trip back since that day in the late 1970s when the guard barred the door. She chuckled to herself as she entered the building. How times have changed.

Abby hearkens back to a similar insult she suffered in the old days in Baltimore, home base for T. Rowe Price. This time at another luncheon meeting, where Abby was hosting a gathering that had a former White House chief economist among its guests. It was the middle of summer in balmy Baltimore. In that neck of the woods, summer days can get not only unbearably hot, but also unbearably humid. At this luncheon meeting, the exclusive club's air conditioner broke down, leaving the lunch guests to melt in 92° heat. The maitre d' refused to move the group to a cooler spot in the club because Abby was a member of the party.

These days, there are very few who would insult Abby Joseph Cohen like that. Like the cigarette commercial said, "You've come a long way baby."

Greed, Gaming, and Trickery

A s we are taught in capitalism school, Wall Street is a place where businesses raise money. Whether through the sale of stock to public investors or by selling bonds in an effort to borrow funds, companies finance their future expansion on Wall Street.

In a perfect world, this would be a tidy process, devoid of conflicts, corruption, or fraud. Needless to say, we do not live in a perfect world. And, Wall Street as a microcosm of the world in which we live, is not a perfect place. In fact, one could argue that Wall Street is a world unto itself, where the normal influences of life are magnified. Where fear and greed are the driving forces, rather than little voices inside our heads.

And at times, the economic system the Street houses is misused and abused. Here are the tales of some small abuses that, while not hugely corrupt like the excesses of the 1980s, very well illustrate the conflicts all investors face when wheeling and dealing on Wall Street.

Tall Tales

The money management and investment advisory businesses are brutally competitive. Investors are constantly clamoring for higher and higher returns, regardless of the investment climate. The pressure to perform, like a groom on his wedding night, is a pressure that haunts money managers, traders, and investors day in and day out. Investment professionals live with performance anxiety for their entire lives.

Sometimes investment professionals stretch the truth a little bit when it comes to publicizing their investment results. Some claim to have never had a down year. Others say they are among the most highly ranked players on the Street. Sometimes the claims are true. Other times, they are partially true. And still other times, these claims border on fraud.

Some professionals stretch the truth because they are always hungry for new investment dollars. The bigger the pool of money managed, the bigger the fees they collect for managing it. The better the performance, the greater amount of money that flows through the door. It's a vicious circle that demands money managers look great at all times, in the short term and in the long term.

The performance of Wall Street professionals is tracked in a variety of ways. Money managers are "graded" quarterly, simply by how much their investment funds are up or down. Industry analysts and market strategists are ranked by a Wall Street magazine known as *The Institutional Investor*. Making the *II* list indicates the popularity of analysts among those for whom they provide investment research. Newsletter writers are ranked by another newsletter writer named Mark Hulbert. He writes the "Hulbert Financial Digest," a monthly letter that tracks the investment recommendations of countless financial newsletters and ranks them according to their short-term and long-term successes. Hulbert was among the first to discover that the proudest boast of all time on Wall Street simply wasn't true.

The performance claim that stands out as most curious, strangely enough, came from one of the industry's most humble players. And it led to a formal investigation by the Securities and Exchange Commission, just recently resolved.

Steven Leeb, a gentle soul, who was a frequent guest on all the major business shows and frequently quoted in the *Wall Street Journal* and elsewhere, was among the most successful newsletter writers in the business. For years he has been editing two widely read letters, "Personal Finance" and "The Big Picture." His letters are read by over 100,000 subscribers nationwide. For many years, Leeb was among the best-performing market prognosticators around, delivering sound investment advice to his subscribers.

But for some unknown reason, Steven slipped up. Not in his performance, but in his performance claims.

In 1993 Leeb's publishers made a wild claim and leveled an even wilder challenge to anyone daring enough to take it. First, they claimed that Leeb's market-timing model turned $10,000 into more than $39 million between 1980 and 1991. The average gain, 99% per year! The publishers then offered a reward of $10,000 to any taker who could prove that he or she had done better in the same period of time. It was a gauntlet that few chose to run.

To achieve his fantastic results, Leeb used an econometric model to time his entrances and exits from the stock market. The model was a stunning model of success, without equal anywhere else in the financial universe. The February 15, 1993, edition of *Forbes Magazine* noted, "Not even Warren Buffett has come close to (making) 390,000% in that decade." Leeb's publishing company noted publicly that if any investor would have followed Leeb's market-tested advice, they would have gotten filthy rich in only eleven years.

The first observer to look into Leeb's claims was Mark Hulbert. His findings immediately deflated the claim. Hulbert first showed that Leeb had revised his econometric model several times over the years, so the model used in the boast was not even remotely similar to the model on which Leeb had based his actual earlier recommendations. Further, to achieve the astounding results Leeb back-tested the model to see how it would have done had the revised model been employed since 1981. Hulbert cried foul.

Leeb's real recommendations, long tracked by Hulbert, did not match the back-tested data Leeb and his publisher used for the print ads. To make matters worse, for an investor to have actually achieved the 390,000% increase in his portfolio, he would have had to have been 500% long at all times. That means an investor would have used borrowed money to pyramid the gains. In other words it would have taken five times the amount of money in the existing portfolio to have chalked up the advertised gains.

Now here's the real quirky part of the deal. In his investigation, Hulbert found that Leeb never recommended going 500% long. In fact, some of his real recommendations from prior years contradicted the advice offered in the revised, back-tested model. And the strange thing about all this is that Leeb's real track record was always quite impressive and not much in need of embellishment. The gains from his real advice placed him among the most successful investment advisors around. His model portfolio was up 160% in the years between 1988 and 1993, according to Hulbert. Leeb sported gains nearly unmatched by other newsletter writers who had been around as long as he had.

For his own account, Leeb always claimed that he did not review the advertising done by the company that publishes his letter. He just edited the letter, he said, and worried little about letter-writing logistics.*

A lesson for investors: Past performance (particularly when it's fabricated) is not indicative of future results! At least that's what they say in financial ads.

Gaming the Market

Wall Street, by and large, is generally on the up-and-up. The markets are mostly fair and the pricing of stocks and bonds is usually efficient. But, not always. There are still times, as in the olden days of robber barons, stock-jobbers, and bucket shops, that someone tries to do a put-up in the stock market. Every once in a while, a market trader will get caught in an illicit scheme to mark a stock up or down in an effort to gain a little advantage. Insider trading is still very much a common occurrence and regulators still haven't completely eradicated fraud, bid-rigging, and

---

*Without admitting or denying guilt, Leeb and his investment group settled charges of false advertising and paid the SEC $300,000 in January 1996.

outright theft of public funds by scam artists and charlatans. Quite frankly, those illegal activities will always be with the markets, no matter how hard regulators try to regulate or market participants try to police themsclves. It's the way of Wall Street. Fear and greed are simply too prevalent to irradicate illegal acts.

In the market's not-too-distant past, things were even worse. In the early years of this century bucket shops, the early form of brokerage operations, routinely fleeced the public out of its hard-earned money. Bucket shops fostered gambling, not investing. Back then bucket shop owners frequently pushed up a stock's price, to lure in unsuspecting suckers who were promptly separated from their funds as the stock plunged in value. The bucketeers kept the margin that individual investors put up to "buy" the stock and profited quite handsomely from the little game.

Back then, such a maneuver was called "painting the tape." Today, it is called "gaming the market."

In June of 1993, the big interests had their way with the market in a manner that was more reminiscent of the 1920s than the 1990s. On the third Friday of June, 1993, several large Wall Street firms engaged in a classic ramp, bidding up stock prices artificially, only to unload millions of shares on an unsuspecting public, with no time to go in that day's trading game.

But first, a little history. The third Friday of every month is a fairly significant day for the stock, option, and futures markets. It's the day on which stock options expire. Stock options are derivative contracts, based on the value of underlying stocks, or stock indexes. Call options, on either stocks or stock indexes, allow traders to buy one hundred shares of a stock, like IBM, or a basket of stocks, like the Standard & Poor's 100 Index, at a preset price by a particular date in the future. Put options allow the trader the right to sell the stock or stock index at a preset price by a future date.

The options allow investors or traders to control a lot of stock with just a little money down. The margins required to buy options or futures are often as little as 5% of the contract's value. To buy stocks, investors must put down half of the value of the stock buy, similarly, on margin. Because of the relative cheapness of options, investors use them as hedging tools against their stock holdings. Options trade on options exchanges and the contracts expire monthly. There are options on individual stocks and options on stock indexes. Futures contracts are similar to options, but they are used solely as a proxy for stock indexes like the Standard & Poor's 500. The futures contracts also allow traders or investors to control a basket of stocks at a fraction of the cost of purchasing all of the stocks in the basket.

The developments of options and futures has led to some very arcane trading strategies known as arbitrage-related program trading and portfolio insurance—two big factors in the 1987 stock market crash. The proliferation of stock options, stock index options, and stock index futures led to a great deal of hedging and speculating in the options and futures markets in the 1980s, activity that greatly increased the complexity of investing. The markets have not been the same since.

Now, these complex strategies using stocks, stock options, and stock index futures frequently led to bouts of volatility in the stock market. The now-failed strategy of portfolio insurance helped precipitate the crash of 1987. It was a silly notion based on the assumption one could endlessly sell stock index futures contracts to protect one's stock portfolio, without causing a ripple effect in the underlying market. It was a notion from which everyone was disabused on October 19, 1987. On that fateful today, fearful investors dumped futures contracts with reckless abandon, hoping that by shorting the futures they could profit on those sales, even as their underlying portfolios shrunk in value. However, that activity just made matters worse. By the end of the day, the Dow Jones Industrials was down 508 points, or 22%, the largest one-day decline in market history. It represented a failure of many investors to understand the complicated mechanics of derivative markets and their unique power to influence the liquidity of the underlying market. However, some traders and investors understand all too well how to use these powerful tools, as we will soon see.

In the aftermath of the crash, the Securities and Exchange Commission, the New York Stock Exchange, the Chicago Mercantile Exchange, and the Chicago Board Options Exchange all put into place various restrictions on many of the complex transactions that involved stocks, stock options, and stock index futures. This forced big players to more clearly disclose how their transactions were constructed and how they planned to unwind their strategies when options and futures expired at month or quarter-end.

The monthly expiration of stock options and stock index options were routine enough, even in the heyday of program trading and portfolio insurance, back in the 1980s. But the third Friday of each quarter was, quite frequently, an unusually hectic day as big institutions "unwound" some very large, very complicated transactions involving all three types of vehicles in the final minutes of trading. The trades required to complete some of these complex transactions occurred as the market closed—the final hour of trading that in the 1980s came to be known as the Triple Witching Hour.

Because so many investors undertook huge options-related programs, the closing out of those arcane trades caused some very wild gyrations in the market. As billions of dollars worth of transactions were completed, enormous surges in the volume of stock, options, and futures contracts became evident in the final minute of the day. The players were capturing big profits they'd earned earlier in the quarter, capitalizing on the inevitable discrepancies in the prices of underlying stocks, the options on those stocks, and the associated futures contracts. The prices of all three instruments would converge in the final moment of that triple witching hour in a wild orgy of profit-taking that sometimes terrorized even the most seasoned Wall Street traders.

After the crash, market regulators tried to tone down those activities. To prevent market participants from being surprised by the huge buy or sell orders associated with the unwinding of those complicated strategies described earlier, big players were asked to show what stocks they had to buy or sell in the final hour and the size of their so-called market-on-close orders.

Publication of those market-on-close orders allowed the specialists on the floor of the New York Stock Exchange to find buyers for huge blocks of stock for sale or sellers for huge blocks of stock to buy. Specialists match buyers and sellers of stocks, a job made particularly difficult by expiration, since huge buy or sell orders raced through the system on triple witching Fridays. The publication of intentions to buy or sell was designed to make the market more orderly on options expiration Fridays and on the quarterly triple witching.

From 1988 to September of 1993, the big players disclosed their intentions several times throughout the last hour of trading, showing how much stock they had to buy or sell. The NYSE would put out a list of stocks that had buy or sell order in imbalances of 50,000 shares or more. Sometimes firms would have millions of shares of a WalMart, General Electric, or Exxon to buy or sell at the close of trading. In the final hour, the specialists would use the list to match up buyers and sellers of the big blocks, to smooth out the volatility that often came from such big transactions.

After a couple years of publishing the intentions and subsequent order imbalances, some traders found new ways to capitalize on the expected rush hour. If a trader saw that many firms needed to buy a million shares of Wal-Mart at day's end, he might buy the stock before the close to ride the stock up as the inevitable buying pressure drove WalMart shares substantially higher. Some stocks would jump a dollar a share in the final minutes of trading, thanks to the surge of activity in the stocks. Conversely, some stocks would fall by that much if there were millions of shares for sale.

Basically, the piggybackers would buy the stocks the big guys were buying or sell the stocks the big guys were selling. By the early 1990s even individual investors would try to earn a couple bucks scalping stocks in the final hour of trading as they saw (on FNN and, later, on CNBC) what the big guys were up to.

Well, no game that easy lasts forever. On the third Friday of June 1993, the big guys decided to make a few bucks off the little guys, who had been riding their coattails, free of charge, for a number of expirations.

On that day, most everyone on Wall Street was expecting another routine triple witching Friday, in which the big guys would close out their complicated transactions in the final hour, announcing what they had to buy or sell, shortly after 3 P.M. eastern time. Ironically, by this time, the expirations had become quite routine. The specialists did a good job pairing off buyers and sellers, and the volatility that used to be associated with these events began to die down.

But this day was to be a bit different. A put-up job was in the works. Several large firms submitted fake buy orders of millions of shares of stock in WalMart, Merck (the big drug company), and Exxon. Seemingly savvy traders and a few individual investors who were too smart for their own good, jumped on the quarterly gravy train, hoping to ride those stocks to a quick profit as the big traders closed out their trades, buying those stocks back in the final minutes of action, as they needed to. As stated, the temporary upward pressure could push those stocks up a point or more in the last hour of action. An easy buck a share in an hour is not a bad rate of return, even for the little guy. But the big guys knew better. After publishing phony intentions in the first few minutes of the hour, the piggybackers pushed up the prices of the aforementioned stocks even further.

Lo and behold, the big guys started dumping the stocks they purportedly wanted to buy. Public investors were faked out and left owning the stocks that, in reality, the big guys wanted to sell, not buy! The unexpected maneuver caused the Dow Jones average to drop 20 points in the last minute of trading as the presumed buying pressure disappeared and was replaced with massive orders to sell stocks at the close of the day.

Investors were understandably angry. Some called the offices of CNBC, the business television station to complain about the shenanigans. They had been burned, now holding stocks that were suddenly worth less than they paid for them, and for no good reason, other than the fact that the big guys "set them up."

A CNBC anchor who fielded some of the calls and looked into the matter, called one of his best sources on the floor of the New York Stock Exchange. PaineWebber's Art Cashin, a veteran floor broker on the NYSE, tipped him off to what had actually happened. He called it "gaming the market." The anchor promptly did several reports about the put-up job on the Big Board, as did Tom Cochran, of *Barron's*, the weekly financial magazine. The stories prompted the NYSE to alter the rules at expiration, allowing the big guys only one, not several, chances to announce their intentions on expiration Fridays. That rule kept the biggies from setting up public investors.

The market hasn't been manipulated that way since. One of Wall Street's oldest players, who has seen a few manipulations in his day aptly notes, "The game never changes. Only the people do!"

Free Willy

In the ivory towers of academia, finance professors have long sought the secrets of the stock market. They toil away in their laboratories, making market models that show just how the stock market works. They present their theories with great fanfare and much pride, having figured out just what makes Wall Street tick. But, despite all the academic pronouncements about how Wall Street really works, there are many competing theories, each of which has many adherents and many detractors.

Most of the studies are dreadfully boring and lack any of the dynamism that exists in the world of investing itself. One study claims the stock market is highly rational at all times while another says that investing is nothing more than a random walk through time. Whether you subscribe to the efficient market theory, or the random walk theory, there is only one certainty about academic studies of Wall Street—most ivory tower finance professors haven't a clue as to how the stock market really works.

And here's a great example of why that's true (particularly for those who hold that the stock market is highly efficient and almost always rational).

Many years ago Sea World, the aquatic amusement theme park, was a publicly traded company that was an extremely popular spot for parents to take the kids on a sunny weekend in Southern California. Its shares rose and fell on the popularity of its various shows that featured Shamu, the killer whale or Orca, another killer creature. As its theme park attendance rose and fell, so did its profits, just like any other entertainment business. Today, Sea World is a small part of a larger company, but many years ago it was, as we said, a stand-alone entity.

It so happens that in the mid-1970s a couple of Wall Street traders turned bearish (or whalish, if you will) on Sea World's future prospects. Theme park attendance was softening, and they reasoned that the theme of this theme park was growing stale. Short-term traders who think a company's business is turning sour will "short" the company's stock. A short sale is a bet that a stock will decline over time. In a short sale, the trader borrows the stock, sells it, and hopes to buy it back more cheaply at a later date. The trader then pockets the difference.

So, these two traders—now simply hating Sea World's business prospects and its stock—sold short 50,000 shares of Sea World. It was, they hoped, going to be a profitable trade. Unfortunately for them the tide turned, so to speak, and the stock rose considerably in a very short time. They found themselves faced with swelling losses. In fact, one day the stock jumped four dollars a share, sticking them with a $200,000 loss just for that day. One of the traders called his partner, desperate for help on this money-losing trade.

"Peter, we're short 50,000 of Sea World, up 4. What the hell are we supposed to do?"

"Hold on. I'll get back to you," Peter snapped.

Picking up the phone, he called a contact at the brokerage firm he had known quite well over the years. The firm had underwritten Sea World's sale of stock to the public.

"Orca's sick," was all Peter had to say, hanging up the phone and waiting for the market to respond. It did with a flourish, as Sea World shares dove like a bottom-fisher in a feeding frenzy. The stock was suddenly down $5 on the day, instead of up $4.

Peter's partner called back.

"We covered the short. But we bought 20,000 shares at the bottom. What do we do now?"

"Hold on," Peter snapped again. Dialing back his buddy, Peter said, "Sorry, bad information. Orca's OK."

The stock quickly rebounded. It ended the day with a gain. So did Peter and his partner.

Remember, the next time someone tells you the market is efficient, think of it as another Wall Street fish story.

A Banker's Tale

Investment banking is a relationship business. Investment bankers are different than brokers and traders though they rely on both to facilitate deals. They help American corporations sell stocks and bonds, make acquisitions, restructure operations, and provide a host of different financial functions for clients. Investment bankers are Wall Street's dealmakers. As the rainmakers of the Street, they rank among the elite in lower Manhattan.

Frequently on Wall Street there's open warfare, when the needs or desires of investment bankers clash with those of their clients. Let's say a banker wants to do business for a client, while also representing that client's biggest rival. There is a very good chance the banker's desire to generate some additional profits for his firm will go unmet. Sometimes it's the client that wants a particular banker to handle its business. But oftentimes the banker simply can't handle the transaction without losing the business of another important firm that utilizes his services as well. In short, life on Wall Street is filled with inherent conflicts—conflicts that aren't always resolved to everybody's satisfaction.

Greed, Gaming, and Trickery

Take Kirk Kerkorian's 1995 attempt to take over the Chrysler Corporation. Kerkorian, the Las Vegas-based billionaire who made his fortune in casinos and movies, sought the help of Bear Stearns and other major New York City commercial banks to help finance the $22.8 billion bid. Had it been completed, the buyout of Chrysler would have been the second largest such deal in U.S. history, almost as rich as the $25 billion buyout of RJR Nabisco by Kohlberg, Kravis & Roberts. But published reports of the time showed how Chrysler made it clear that any firm offering aid to the enemy would itself become an enemy and lose out on the lucrative investment banking business that the nation's third largest auto company had to offer. No doubt a host of Wall Street firms would have loved to have done a deal that size. The fees would have been staggering and the prestige of doing so large a deal is priceless in terms of free advertising. But Bear Stearns and the New York banks backed away, unwilling to burn a client as powerful and prestigious as Chrysler. And it didn't even matter that seventy-three-year-old legend Lee Iacocca was on Kerkorian's team.

A Morgan Stanley executive recalls a similar conflict between Ford and General Motors, which caught the respectable old-line firm square in the middle. This tale is quite instructive when it comes to demonstrating how Wall Street really works.

The executive harkens back to the 1950s, when Ford, the nation's second largest auto company was still a privately held concern. For all its history as a model of capitalism, Ford remained a private company for nearly forty years after Henry Ford invented mass production. The

97

founder's family, which still controlled a huge chunk of stock in the 1950s, wanted to reap the rewards of its ancestor's efforts by selling a portion of that stake to the public. By cashing out some of its holdings, the Ford Foundation could "monetize" its investment, in other words, it could pull down some pretty hefty pocket change in an initial public offering of stock. To accomplish that transaction, the Ford Foundation sought the help of Morgan Stanley, one of Wall Street's premier investment banks.

Now back then, Morgan Stanley generally did business for General Motors. Ford's principal investment banker of the time was Goldman Sachs. Nonetheless, when the Ford Foundation wanted to sell some stock, it required the top-tier firms to help underwrite the offering.

So, as the story goes, John Young, a principal at Morgan Stanley rang up Fred Donner of GM.

"Fred," he said, "the Ford Foundation is going to sell stock. The Foundation, Fred, not the company. The company's going to cooperate, but the Foundation is selling the stock, and we've been asked to be a manager (of the underwriting). "Would that cause a problem for you?"

Fred's voice came calmly across the line. "It won't cause a problem for me, John. Might cause a problem for you."

And so Morgan Stanley opted out of the offering of Ford Foundation stock. Simple as that. A one-line response from a senior GM official locked Morgan Stanley out of an extremely lucrative stock underwriting, principally because it was being done for a rival firm. That's how this stuff works. As the Morgan Stanley executive remembers, it would have been great to do business with the heirs of the nation's second largest auto company, but GM was bigger. And that was that.

A Trumped-Up Tale

The brokerage community is full of conflicts. Throughout the history of the industry its members have asked whether it's the customer or the firm that comes first. Is a broker really a customer's man, or does he get rich by making his customer "broker?" The questions are asked every day on Wall Street, by the firms, by their clients, by regulators, and by the financial press.

By and large, the men and women of Wall Street are an honorable lot in a sometimes dishonest profession. As in any other business, some players cut corners, some try to get rich quick, while others do right by their clients and aid them in the process of building up their nest eggs. However, there are conflicts in the brokerage business that never get resolved in the client/firm relationship.

Marvin Roffman runs Roffman, Miller, a Philadelphia-based broker-dealer that handles retail investment accounts, from high-net worth clients to semiaverage Joe's looking for some help in planning their financial futures. Roffman caters to the little guy. But Marvin was not always running his own show. Not too long ago he was a vice president of research at the Philadelphia firm, Janney Montgomery Scott. There he was employed as a research analyst, poring over the books of gaming companies, hotels, casinos, recreation, and leisure-time firms.

The business of gaming is, in and of itself, interesting. Calculating the "win percentage," witnessing the construction of new casinos or new riverboats is a big, glamorous business with big dollars at stake. And the people in the industry—from Steve Wynn to Donald Trump to Kirk

99

Kerkorian—make a colorful cast of characters worthy of any big screen glitz and glamour saga.

For many years, Marvin Roffman relished his job as an observer of the gaming scene. He met a lot of wonderful people, stayed at some really wild places, and had a little fun in Sin City every once in a while. But, it was not *all* fun and games. In fact, in a now legendary encounter with "The Donald," Marvin Roffman's relationship with "fun and games" came to a crashing end.

The story Roffman tells clearly illustrates the conflicts of interest inherent on Wall Street. As a well-respected research analyst, it was Roffman's job to make sure investors weren't just rolling the dice when it came to buying the stocks or bonds of gaming companies—except in one case.

In 1989 Donald Trump billed his Taj Mahal casino in Atlantic City the eighth wonder of the modern world. The Taj was billed as a luxury palace that would bring gamblers in droves to the Las Vegas of the east. It was, in Donald Trump's estimation, a sure bet. But to Marvin Roffman the only sure thing about its bonds was that they were going to go bust.

Roffman wondered out loud and quite publicly how The Donald was going to pay a 14% interest rate on Taj Mahal bonds that were floated to finance the construction of this grand casino. After having completed extensive analysis of the Taj Mahal's financial prospects, Roffman decided that there was no way the Taj would do well enough to pay back the bondholders and still keep the casino in the black. So, in June of 1989, he decided against recommending Taj Mahal bonds as an investment to Janney Montgomery Scott clients. Roffman also told the *Wall Street Journal* that the Taj Mahal bonds were a "sell." There was no way Trump could pay the first interest payment given the astounding economic assumptions that were made in the investment prospectus.

The *Wall Street Journal* published his negative comments in March 1990, causing a rather large stir on Wall Street and in Trump's executive suite. Ironically, Roffman had an appointment to see a Trump executive that very day. They were scheduled to discuss, again, the future prospects for the Taj. As soon as he arrived, the executive, who headed up Donald's Atlantic City casino empire, had Marvin thrown off the property. And that was just for starters.

Now here's where the story gets really interesting. An incensed Donald threatened to sue Janney Montgomery Scott, demanding that Roffman apologize for this financial analysis. Trump cried foul, claiming that Roffman's analysis was flawed and that the Taj would immediately live up to its grand billing.

But Roffman refused to retract his statements. He firmly believed the Taj Mahal bonds were a major bust.

But his boss would not have any of that. He sided with Trump and called Roffman's bluff, demanding that he retract his statements and recommend the bonds as an investment. Roffman was also required to deliver a presentation to the company's sales force, written by other people, touting the Taj.

His boss demanded Roffman sign on to a report claiming the Taj Mahal would be the greatest success ever. At that point his supervisor, asked,

"Marvin, can you live with this report?"

To which Roffman replied, "Live with it? These bonds are going to go bust!"

Tom stated flatly, "I didn't ask you that. Can you live with this thing?"

Roffman remembers that his supervisors simply wanted the whole controversy to just go away. And there was only one way that would happen—if Marvin capitulated and recommended the bonds. They were more frightened of Donald Trump than they were of their clients losing money on his bonds.

Roffman recalls the words of warning of his one-time supervisor:

"Janney Montgomery Scott is a wholly owned subsidiary of Penn Mutual Life Insurance Company. Life insurance companies don't like waste. They don't like negatives. They don't like potential lawsuits. So I don't want to see any more negatives again!"

He then threatened to take Roffman's responsibilities in the gaming group away from him unless he played the game Trump's way.

Roffman refused. Trump bellowed loudly and threatened again to sue. Roffman was fired.

The Taj Mahal missed its first interest payment on October 15, 1990. It eventually went bankrupt and was forced to restructure its debt obligations at more manageable rates of interest.

Roffman sued Janney Montgomery and won a large cash settlement award in arbitration. He sued The Donald and settled out of court for an undisclosed sum. He made enough money from both lawsuits to start his own firm and live comfortably as an entrepreneur.

Greed, Gaming, and Trickery

Two No-Trump

R on Baron is one of Wall Street's most noted money managers, handling over $800 million of other people's money and investing it exclusively in the stock market. Graying a bit, but still lean, as in his youth, Baron is a fixture of the financial scene, frequently appearing in a financial magazine that shares his name (*Barron's*). Like Marvin Roffman, Ron Baron also worked at Janney Montgomery Scott (JMS). Early in his career, Ron talked his way into a position at Janney, where he helped create the brokerage's very first research department. Back in 1970 Janney Montgomery had 250 brokers but no research department and, therefore, no data to help them sell stock to the public. A gentleman by the name of Tony Tabell did the only research the firm undertook. He analyzed stock market charts, using their price histories to determine the likely future course of stock prices, both for individual stocks and for the market as a whole. But at that time no one at JMS analyzed the fundamental health of the companies in which JMS bought or sold shares. Ron Baron was first to do that.

Ron's first assignment was to crisscross the country every week to familiarize himself with the operations of companies in whose stock Janney clients might like to invest. So every Monday Ron boarded a plane and headed for parts unknown, coming back with a dossier on two or three companies. And each week he'd discuss their prospects in a letter to JMS brokers who, in turn, would pitch the stocks to eager investors.

103

Traders' Tales

That's how the system works today, just as it did twenty-five years ago. In fact research, while not always unbiased, is a very valuable tool in the investment profession. And there are a host of well-respected analysts on the Street. They, like all professionals, face inevitable conflicts in their business, but, by and large, they earn their keep by doing some pretty good work. Some research analysts make over a million dollars a year today. In turn, they help the firm sell that research to clients, either as stand-alone research reports purchased by professional money managers or in the form of investment advice for mom-and-pop investors. The more the clients like the work of a Wall Street research analyst, the higher his or her compensation.

After about a year of traveling, gathering research, and combining his fundamental analysis with the technical tools of his colleague, Tony Tabell, Ron Baron took a flier on his own. He had been doing a great deal of work on a real estate development company called General Development (GD). Baron grew disenchanted with the firm's future prospects and felt confident the company's profit picture was about to dim. He felt that its stock was about to nosedive. Stock prices often decline sharply when the profit outlook sours. Any advance reckoning of such a deterioration is of great help to a brokerage house's stable of investors who can, and will, exit the stock before it heads into a free fall.

Confident that General Development's outlook was rapidly deteriorating, Baron penned a negative letter about the firm, circulating it widely to his network of brokers—even giving it to *Barron's*, the weekend financial magazine that has been known to have a large impact on the stock prices.

Greed, Gaming, and Trickery

As Ron Baron remembers, the Monday morning after *The Wall Street Transcript* panned the stock based on Baron's analysis, shares of General Development tumbled, falling about $3 a share to $34. As Ron walked into his office that day, it was abuzz. General Development, in addition to being a troubled company with an uncertain future, was also a major client of Janney Montgomery Scott.

As soon as he arrived at work, Baron was informed of a waiting phone call. It was the chairman of General Development. Needless to say, Ron quickly picked up the phone.

"What are you talking about? You don't know what you're doing . . . ." And some other unprintable comments followed. The chairman was screaming at Baron for his comments that found their way into the pages of *The Wall Street Transcript*. After his tirade, the exasperated executive hung up on Ron. But the onslaught did not end there. The chairman's call was followed by one from GD's president. Same hollering. Same result—a slammed-down receiver.

At this point, the area outside Ron's office filled with commotion. Baron remembers hearing the sound of slamming doors accompanying the sound of slamming phones. He recalls being treated to a concerto in slam. The thundering was almost as ominous as the opening strains of Beethoven's Fifth. Boom-boom, boom-boom. Doors were opening and then slamming shut throughout the offices of Janney Montgomery Scott.

Moments later, Ron was summoned into the office of JMS chairman, Edgar Scott.

"Ron, we love you and we think you do great work. But you messed up a General Development underwriting we were going to participate in. You just wrote a negative report about a client of the firm. Now they're threatening to sue us. We can't stand the pressure, and we've got to fire you. You've got to be out of here by noon."

That was Ron's reward for alerting investors to the newest developments at General Development. In a way, like Marvin Roffman, Ron had the last laugh. The big real estate firm went bankrupt. Ron, however, never got his job back, but he moved on to bigger and better things.

Flash forward about nineteen years. Ron Baron was leafing through the newspaper only to read that Marvin Roffman suffered a similar fate at his former place of employment, Janney Montgomery Scott. Baron called Roffman to commiserate. Shortly thereafter, Roffman's lawyer called Baron. Their conversation helped pave the way for Marvin Roffman's several hundred-thousand-dollar settlement.

As on the roulette wheel, so too on Wall Street, what goes around, comes around.

Get It in Writing

The best lessons in life are free. At least that's what everyone hopes when starting out in a new career. For Ron Baron, now a renowned figure on Wall Street, his first and best lesson about doing business came cheap. Baron is not a market-timer, that is, someone concerned with whether stocks are in a bullish or bearish cycle. He's a stock picker, a bottoms-up analyst who prides himself on making winning picks in the equity market. He buys stocks he thinks will double in three years. (Don't we all?)

Greed, Gaming, and Trickery

Ron began his career on Wall Street after deciding it was a much more interesting place to be than law school, which is where he went right from college. But for Ron, practicing law was a bit too pedantic, studying cases and filing briefs would not turn out to be his life's passion. The one side benefit to law school, though, was it kept Ron out of the army, which was almost everyone else's alternative education institution in the late 1960s.

As soon as the draft had officially passed him by Ron came to Wall Street. He was prodded by an uncle who had stimulated Baron's interest by recommending what are now classic investing books, one of which was by the fabled technical analyst, Joe Granville. In the 1960s Joe Granville was just beginning to make a name for himself as a market chartist, a technician who looks at how a stock has traded historically to determine how it will trade in the future. A few pages on the easy way to riches and Ron was hooked.

But it wouldn't be quite that easy. Baron struggled to find a job in his early days on the Street. He had $600 in cash and was in debt $13,000 from his law school days. Not a pretty balance sheet for someone who would one day read balance sheets for a living.

But eventually he landed a post as a research assistant. He became quite skilled quite quickly. Some of Wall Street's most prominent investors relied on the stock by stock information that Baron and a long-time friend and partner were providing. So skilled in fact, that in 1975 other firms began courting them with offers of money, perquisites, and status. One firm, Herzfeld and Stern (H&S), was particularly aggressive in its courtship of Ron and his partner.

Steven Seiden, a senior player at H&S, badgered the boys incessantly with offers, calling every day at their offices, calling at home, calling at midnight with promises of a profitable new venture.

Seiden routinely sent the limo to get Baron and his buddy to visit, rolling out the red carpet treatment for the two up-and-coming analysts. For weeks this courtship pressed on. Lunch at the firm's headquarters was routine. So was the car and driver. All the while Seiden showered the pair with praise for their insightful work and stable full of high-profile clients. They were wined and dined in a manner befitting royalty. The flattery finally worked. After a few months of limousine rides and heavy petting, the two analysts decided to go all the way. They accepted the proposal.

Ron Baron called Steve Seiden to seal the deal.

"OK, Steve. We're going to join. We're going to come to Herzfeld and Stern. We'll start in June."

Steve was quite pleased with their decision and once again, the limo was waiting to take them to their new home to sign the appropriate paperwork. In fact, that car and driver had become a routine feature of the courtship. They grew to expect it and simply assumed it would be a permanent feature of their new employment. Call it a perk, befitting what they had become—Wall Street stars!

As they headed for H&S, the pair was excited and honored by the star treatment. When they arrived at Herzfeld they were ushered into the office of Paul Cohen, the senior partner of the firm, who was housed in a cavernous oak-paneled and plush den.

Cohen welcomed them aboard.

"It's so good to have you boys here," he said, "We're going to do great business together. This is the firm for you!"

They signed the deal and were ushered out. When they got downstairs, the limo had vanished. It was nowhere in sight.

Baron learned that very moment, if you don't have it in writing, you don't have it at all—no matter how important you think you are.

Full Faith and Credit

Every Monday, except for holidays, the U.S. government borrows money. It does so by selling three- and six-month Treasury bills. On an average Monday, the Treasury might sell $23–26 billion of the short-term debt paper to finance its ongoing operations. These bills pay interest to their holders. But unlike bonds, the interest payments aren't actually mailed out to the investors. Instead, the bills are discounted from a face value of 100 to reflect the going rate of interest. For example, if a Treasury bill yields a 5% rate of interest, the Treasury would sell the bill for $95 for every $100 in face value. At the end of thirty, sixty, or ninety days, depending on the maturity date, the Treasury refunds the entire $100. The investor earns 5% on the money. Simple as that.

Many professional traders and investors use U.S. Treasury bills as a safe haven investment. The three-month government debt obligations are, for all intents and purposes, riskless investments that offer a reasonable rate of return for short-term funds. Many large speculators, investors, traders and even individual investors park their funds in T-bills until they decide where to make longer-term commitments. But in the interim they can earn 3, 4, or 5% on their money without the risk of losing a cent.

These days, interestingly enough, no one who buys a T-bill actually gets to touch one. The old Treasury certificates that used to be delivered to T-bill buyers are now out of touch. No longer can anyone ever hold one of those intricately designed certificates in their hot little hands.

Jim Benham, the chairman of the Benham family of mutual funds, explains how possessing the actual T-bills, themselves, became illegal. As you might guess, a few cleverly engineered scams took T-bill certificates out of circulation for the general public.

By way of background, Benham runs a family of mutual funds now owned by Franklin Resources, another major mutual fund company. He left Merrill Lynch in his very early days in the business to start his own fund firm from scratch. After nearly twenty years of hard work, he built it into a powerhouse that catered to individual investors who wanted to buy bonds or bond funds. He took advantage of the consumer's desire to pay only small fees to purchase mutual fund investments. Like a financial Sam Walton, Jim Benham made money in a discount financial warehouse. And in catering to that clientele, Jim built his company into a firm with $14 billion in assets before selling it to Franklin for $50 million. Benham, himself, is reportedly worth $100 million.

A quietly confident man, he is an astute student of markets and economics. He studies charts of bonds, inflation trends, and economic indicators in an effort to better understand the investment climate of the bond market. Lest you think all work and no play makes Jim a very dull boy, he is also a savvy musician, for years the lead trombone player with the Full Faith and Credit Orchestra, a swing band.

Jim Benham is also an avid fan of storytelling. Always ready with some comic relief, he frequently regales clients or journalists with the latest humorous bits that spring from the trading desks and pits across the country. He also has some compelling recollections of market history that are as interesting as any of Wall Street's latest jokes. Here's one that explains why, today, no one can get their hands on an actual Treasury certificate.

In 1976 the U.S. government stopped delivering T-bill certificates to investors because of a wily fraud easily perpetrated by any T-bills holder. It was a fraud, Jim Benham recalls, that allowed investors to get all the interest paid from a T-bill without paying any taxes on their investments.

The scam was a simple strategy employed by wealthy investors or anyone willing to buy a lot of T-bills and then fly to Switzerland. The Treasury department used to deliver $8\frac{1}{2}$-by-11-inch certificates to all T-bill purchasers from the government's weekly auctions. These certificates were denominated first in $10,000 pieces of paper. Then $100,000. Then $1 million. Then $10 million. All the certificates were payable to the bearer of the bills. Smart investors, who knew quite well the tax laws of the day, would put their bearer bills in an envelope and address the envelope to themselves. They would then stuff the envelopes into their breast pockets and head for the airport. Grabbing a flight to Zurich, they would then have a Swiss bank set up a numbered account (one with only a number, not a name attached) and let the bank collect the proceeds from their T-bill investments. The money went into the numbered account, which could not be traced back to the U.S. customer. So the bearer never paid any taxes to the government.

The maneuver bypassed the laws in this country that forbade the announced transfer of large sums of money across borders. Since none of the detectors at the airport was triggered by a T-bill stuffed in an envelope, investors frequently made off with the goods without ever getting caught. Not a bad deal. A $10 million dollar bill, in 90 days, paying 5% interest would yield $500,000 on an annualized basis, tax-free.

As Benham recalls, there was a companion dodge to that illicit transaction that allowed other savvy investors to avoid paying taxes on T-bill income. To achieve this other scam, investors bought T-bills in the secondary market, rather than at auction. They would then hold the bill until it nearly matured, letting the T-bill increase in value. But before they could be held liable for any taxes on the interest income, the well-heeled investor would sell the bills, collecting most of the accrued interest, but none of the tax liability.

To understand the process, remember that the U.S. Treasury auctions off three- and six-month T-bills every Monday. Investors can buy them directly from the Treasury or the Federal Reserve. The T-bills pay reasonable rates of interest, historically anywhere from 3% to 10%. They are discounted at the auction: Essentially, the interest rate being paid is subtracted from 100. For a 5% T-bill, investors would pay $95 for a $100 T-bill. At the maturity date, three months later, the investor would get $100, earning 5% on his money. The bill, Benham explains, is like an escalator. It rises, incrementally, toward 100 until the it matures, when it is worth exactly 100 cents on the dollar.

Greed, Gaming, and Trickery

Back in the 1970s and before, U.S. tax law stipulated that whomever owned the bill ten days before the maturity date would be responsible for paying taxes on the interest income. Smart investors figured they could sell their T-bills eleven days before maturity. So they'd buy the bills in the secondary market to avoid any official recording of their purchases. Remember, these bills would increase in value as they grew to maturity. Eleven days before that date, though, the bills were worth nearly 100 cents on the dollar. The savvy types sold the bills on the 89th day and never paid taxes.

So, next time you buy a T-bill, ask your broker for the certificate. When he tells you that you can't have it, ask him why. Just for fun.

Investors' Tales

Investors are as different from traders as surgeons are from paramedics. Investors take the long view and do not respond to short-term stimuli. They buy and hold their stocks and commodities, eschewing the frantic, and sometimes antic, behavior of the short-term trader. Although not of the same genus, the two are distant cousins who rely on each other for their business.

Legendary investors, then, are in a league all their own. In the following pages you will meet some of the biggest investing guns of all time. Their tales offer unique insights into the way they think. And while their stories are not nearly as ribald as those of the trading communities, they might be more instructive for the reader looking for a few useful lessons.

These reminiscences show how some of the great investment minds think and how they score in a world that has only a few real winners.

Wall Street, Hollywood-Style

Liam Dalton is one of Wall Street's up-and-coming stars. He currently runs a $450 million money management firm, Axiom Partners, and is among the most successful young investors on the Street. He has movie star good looks and a model wife. He's made a good name and great living for himself managing money and will quite likely rank among the best when all is said and done. In fact, from the perspective of a casual observer, Liam is living the quintessential Wall Street dream.

Liam Dalton spent his high school days as a runner on the floor of the New York Stock Exchange, getting a feel for the market at its very core. He began his professional career in 1983 after leaving college, when he joined Bear Stearns. Like all novice money men, Liam was a retail broker. This includes cold calling from the phone book, building a client base, and earning a reputation. He went on to manage money at the Bear and in two short years he made partner, a stunning feat for someone so recently out of school. In 1988, three years after he made partner, Liam Dalton struck out on his own to form his own money management operation. He's been doing pretty well ever since.

But Dalton still feels that something is missing from his life. Something near and dear to him has been gone since 1985, when he first made partner at Bear Stearns: his trademark red suspenders.

Despite his relative youth, Dalton had a reputation for being a top producer on the Street in his early days at the Bear. One day that year Dalton received a call from Twentieth Century Fox, asking Liam to help out on some technical matters relating to a new film being made with a Wall Street backdrop. The next thing he knew, Liam Dalton was showing Charlie Sheen around the trading room, helping him model the character he would play in Oliver Stone's *Wall Street*.

As Sheen's research for the part intensified, he spent three or four days a week at Dalton's desk, watching him trade and learning the ways of Wall Street. The commotion frequently distracted Liam from the pressing business of the day. Meantime, the girls in the secretarial pool frequently oohed and aahed at the presence of one of Hollywood's most successful and available young stars. Sheen's trading research lasted about two months, after which he went off to shoot the movie.

Here's the rub though. Liam Dalton lent Charlie Sheen his red suspenders, which you may or may not recall, were worn by Sheen in the movie. Liam has yet to get his suspenders back. He even ran into Charlie not too long ago on the ski slopes at Canby Ridge. Charlie says he can't find them. Liam thinks otherwise.

Charlie, if you're reading this, please return the suspenders to Axiom Capital in New York. Liam wants them back!

The Peter (Lynch) Principles

Peter Lynch is among the greatest investors of all time. He has done for mutual funds what Michael Jordan did for basketball or Joe Montana did for football—he raised the entire game to a new level. Like Jordan and Montana, Lynch made investing an art form, and in so doing, captured the attention of a nation of investors and savers. He captured a few dollars, too. But as with any great performer, the money is only a by-product of the performance.

Investors' Tales

Lynch, like Michael Jordan, retired at the top of his game, when his hand was still hot and his services most desired. In 1991, Lynch walked away from the best job in the mutual fund business. Tired of the eighty-hour workweeks and longing to spend more time with his wife and daughters, he gave it all up. It was widely reported at the time that Lynch's father suffered a heart attack and died at a very early age, a stress-related tragedy Lynch hoped not to repeat. So, like any great trader or investor, Lynch took his profits and walked away clean.

But, like Michael Jordan, he did not stay completely retired for long. Lynch is only semiretired today, working as a trustee at Fidelity Investments, the mutual fund company that is home to the fund Lynch built, the flagship Fidelity Magellan Fund. In addition to his trustee duties, Lynch is mentor to many of Fidelity's budding young stars. And he is mentor to not only his own young daughters but also to many underprivileged kids in suburban Boston, where Peter makes his home. He is quite active these days with Boston's Catholic school system, raising money so that disadvantaged youths might profit from a private education. In short, Peter Lynch is still a busy man.

In appearance, Peter Lynch looks a bit like Andy Warhol's long-lost brother. With a big shock of white hair and wire-framed glasses, it appears that he and Warhol might have been separated at birth. And, like Warhol, Lynch achieved more than his fifteen minutes of fame in the financial world. But the similarities end there. Lynch is quiet, unassuming, even shy. He is as modest as Warhol was outrageous.

Peter is known the world over for taking Fidelity Investment's Magellan Fund from a tiny, $20 million fund and turning it into a $14 billion household name that today manages money for 1.1 million individual accounts across the nation. The fund now boasts assets of $53.7 billion (as of January 2, 1996). It has grown by $30 billion since he left only four years ago, a testament to the reputation that Lynch helped build. The fund is now run by a Lynch protégé, Jeffrey Vinik, whom we'll meet in a few pages. But it was Lynch who made Fidelity famous, delivering investment returns nearly unequaled in stock market history while he steered Magellan into uncharted waters.

The Early Days

One of Lynch's most intriguing reminiscences about setting sail with Magellan revolves around the fund's early marketing efforts. Magellan was originally closed to public investors. Its management was taken over by Lynch when the fund was still quite small, with only about $20 million in the pool. Through a few shrewd business moves employed by Fidelity founder Ned Johnson, the fund was merged with other struggling mutual funds, the Essex and Salem funds. The two go-go era refugees were attractive as merger partners only because they had extensive tax-loss carry forwards, an accounting procedure that allows a buyer to use the purchased company's losses to offset future capital gains. The mergers built Magellan into a $100 million fund, at which time Fidelity opened it to public investors. It would later become the most famous mutual fund in the country.

But in its early days, Magellan had few takers. So, as Lynch recalls, Fidelity tried to stimulate a little interest in the fund with a can't miss trick—offering the fund for free. As a marketing gimmick, Fidelity offered Magellan as a no-load fund for its first ninety days in the public arena. In other words, investors would not have to pay the normal fee to have a professional manage their money as they did with other public mutual funds. Curiously, no one at the time seemed all that interested in a free fund.

So the Fidelity folks raised the front management fee, or load, to 2%. Suddenly, the buy orders started coming in. The load was quickly raised to 3%, and investors suddenly went crazy for the fund, snapping up shares of Magellan in a panic, fearful that the load might go even higher. But it did not. And, lo and behold, the first low-load mutual funds in the country were born. Investors were amply rewarded for the purchases in subsequent years. But, believe it or not, many passed up the chance to get the best performing fund of all time for free. Go figure.

Peter's P&L

Peter Lynch has always been best known for his stock-picking ability, rather than stock market timing—a skill he finds somewhat useless since the market continually goes up and down. Peter believes that by picking good common stocks investors can wait out the bad periods in the market and earn solid rates of return on their investments, provided they are in the right stocks at the right time. That's the skill that made Peter famous. Lynch's books have explained to investors everywhere how to buy good common stocks and how to invest for the long haul. Patient attention to detail and a willingness to invest in companies one fully understands can yield astounding investment returns and a promise of a comfortable retirement.

Lynch's famed investment style allowed him to pick some big winners on Wall Street, from Chrysler to the Federal National Mortgage Association (Fannie Mae) to Dunkin' Donuts. And while Peter looked for his stock market loves in, usually, all the right places, he generally liked stocks whose companies operated in his own backyard.

But Lynch admits he sometimes failed to catch rising stars, principally because the companies didn't do business in his native Boston. In fact, many of the companies he failed to invest in are as interesting as those he did ultimately pick.

Peter admits he never bought shares in WalMart, now the nation's largest retailer. The discount department store chain now boasts sales of almost $100 billion a year. Since the stock initially came public, WalMart's early investors have made over thirty-five times their money. Peter never bought it though. WalMart was not a feature of the New England retail landscape. He never went into a WalMart. So he never bought the stock. He doesn't fret about it much though. He lived by his investment credo, buy stocks you know, know stocks you buy. Peter didn't know WalMart.

Peter had the same problem with Home Depot, the big discount home/office supply store, which only recently made its way to the northeastern United States. The upstart chain killed the competition in the home supply business and its stock more than amply rewarded its investors over time. But Peter says he can't tell the difference between a Phillips screwdriver and a hammer. And as Peter Lynch always said, if you don't understand the business or don't know the company, don't buy the stock. Words to remember.

More About Magellan

Jeffrey Vinik is thirty-six years old. He runs the largest mutual fund in the country, Fidelity Investment's flagship Magellan fund. The fund, made famous by Peter Lynch, now boasts assets of about $53 billion. No fund comes even remotely close to it in size. A few have nearly matched its performance over the years, but not many. In terms of sheer size, Fidelity's Magellan is the monster mutual fund of our day, quite possibly of all time.

As for its manager, Jeffrey Vinik, he's a hard working guy with a "bottoms up" approach to investing. That means he doesn't try to time his purchases of stocks to coincide with a bull market. In fact, he doesn't worry as much about the market as a whole as he does about the performance of individual stocks. In many ways, his investment style is like that of his predecessor, Peter Lynch.

Vinik took over in 1992 as only the third manager to run Magellan. He replaced Morris Smith, Peter Lynch's unfortunate successor, who failed to live up to Lynch's past performances. Smith, who took over the fund in mid 1991, was a victim of poor timing, as the successors of many legends are. He began running Magellan in one of the most difficult markets in recent memory. About a year later, he packed his bags and took his family to live in Israel.

121

Jeff Vinik, however, is proving to be a worthy follower of Peter Lynch. In 1995, Vinik quite accurately placed a huge bet on high-technology stocks that were stellar performers in the first half of the year. After some difficult times in 1994, Vinik's performance in 1995 obliterated the fund's four percent decline from the previous year.

For most of his life Jeff Vinik had no interest in the stock market. An engineering major in college, his mathematical mind was leading him away from Wall Street and, in fact, much closer to Main Street. That changed quickly after a summer working for his dad, a trader who invested other people's money. It was a fortuitous internship that led him back to Wall Street, to engage in a little financial engineering that would last the rest of his life. He engineered his way right into becoming the biggest money manager of all time. But that did not happen overnight. After completing college, Vinik went to school at a number of institutions before arriving at Fidelity. He worked as an analyst for Value Line, a venerable old-line research firm that looks into the health of the stock market, company by company. Then he spent time at the trading desk at Donaldson, Lufkin and Jenrette, a Wall Street brokerage. Finally, he made it as a money manager at Fidelity. After distinguishing himself by managing Fidelity's high-flying Contra Fund and the Fidelity Growth and Income Fund, Vinik replaced Morris Smith at Magellan in 1992.

Like Peter Lynch, Vinik is a quiet, unassuming type. He reads a lot of financial statements, talks to a lot of company executives and, finally, makes a lot of investments. He looks a little like Newt Gingrich with dark hair and glasses. But he doesn't share the House Speaker's bombastic personality—

at least not in public. Published reports say the seemingly subdued Vinik is a wild man in the trading room, working fast and furious to get in and out of the stocks that stock the Magellan fund.

The Magellan Fund of today is a bit different from the one Peter Lynch built and ran. It is comprised of about eight hundred different stocks. That's roughly one-third the number of stocks listed on the New York Stock Exchange! The fund has increased in size by almost $40 billion since Peter Lynch stepped down. An amazing growth story.

Jeff Vinik, as you might have guessed, has some thoughts on investing that run a little contrary to conventional Wall Street wisdom. First of all, he believes there are no rules that dictate the ways of Wall Street. Although he looks back at market history to find similarities to the current environment, he also looks for the important differences that might alter a historical pattern in the market and, hopefully, even give him an investment edge. Like Lynch, Jeff Vinik is a stock-picker's stock picker, looking for companies whose earnings growth will explode and drive their stock prices substantially higher.

Apropos of that, he thinks the stocks that become big winners are those that Wall Street has failed to appreciate, those stocks that are not overowned or overfollowed. In other words, Vinik looks for compelling companies whose stories have not yet been recognized by the analytical community on Wall Street. He invests in those, frequently, and watches them become winners. Ultimately those stocks do become overowned and overfollowed, once Wall Street becomes aware of the positive story the company has to tell. Oftentimes that's the signal that the stock has run its course—when the crowd finally piles on.

But Jeff doesn't always sell the stock when it becomes highly regarded. He only sells the stock when the story about the company changes; when the company fails to live up to his rather exacting expectations. Using that strategy he has beaten the Street quite frequently, and that approach allowed him to find L.A. Gear for the Contra Fund and Motorola for Magellan. Jeff swam against the tide on Wall Street, then rode the wave back to shore. In both cases the companies delivered earnings far beyond investors' expectations, for quite some time.

In many respects, Jeff Vinik is something of a contrarian investor, buying stocks that few appreciate, and selling them when too many people know their virtues. Michael Aronstein of West Course Capital summed up that philosophy best when he said, "Conventional wisdom, by its very nature, is useless."

Contrarian investors or traders are not ornery. They don't pick fights with other traders, they don't do things simply to be "contrary." They believe that it's always darkest before the dawn on Wall Street. They invest when there is "blood in the streets." And they "buy 'em when nobody wants 'em." Contrarian investors refuse to be suckered into crowd psychology. They never jump on the bandwagon, nor do they follow the trend. They are not lemmings, they are pioneers. They buy and sell first, and, if they are good, make scads of money by being loners.

Vinik is mostly a contrarian. He recalls a couple stories that illustrate how contrarian investing can work and how it can fail. A true contrarian knows the difference between the times when the crowd is actually right and when it is about to be wrong. A real contrarian buys only when he's sure the crowd is wrong.

Investors' Tales

In the middle 1980s crude oil prices plunged to the lowest levels in over a decade. Prices fell as fast in 1986 as they had risen in 1979, the year of the last great oil shock. Plunging oil prices devastated the domestic oil business in 1986, forcing both big and small U.S. oil companies to cap their small wells in certain oil fields around the country. While the oil patch suffered at the hands of falling prices, the average consumer got a big break on gasoline. We all remember the huge, if only temporary, drop in gasoline prices in 1986. A gallon of gas fell to about seventy-five cents a gallon, reflecting the drop in oil to under ten dollars a barrel.

The crude oil crash was the result of Saudi Arabia's decision to flood the world with crude. It began as an effort to punish other members of the OPEC cartel that had been producing more than their allotted quota of oil. The Saudis, who had played "swing producer" in the cartel, grew tired of cutting their own oil production to support the price of oil on world markets. So, to teach the remaining twelve nations a lesson, Saudi Arabia's then-oil minister, Ahmed Zaki Yamani, threw open the spigot and drove the price of oil through the floor.

And while a lesson was taught to OPEC "cheaters," it also devastated the U.S. oil business. Small wells were capped, domestic exploration and production became unprofitable. The U.S. oil patch dried up. Oil service companies that provided drilling and other oil field equipment sank into a depression not seen for decades. The Texas Panhandle went bust.

Back then Jeff Vinik was following the oil industry at Fidelity Investments. As a student of that industry, Jeff traveled to Texas to meet with executives of large oil service companies, where they briefed him on their company's prospects. Jeff recalls that, in many cases, things had gotten so bad that the executives themselves would turn off the lights and lock the doors when their meeting was over. There were no secretaries and no other support personnel around. Just the CEO who was, basically, left as chief cook and bottle washer, as well as chief executive. It doesn't get much worse than that. And from Jeff's contrary approach to investing, one would assume that such a sight would represent a bottom in the industry and a buying opportunity in the company's stock. But it didn't. Things got worse for a couple more years as oil companies struggled to make ends meet. It took several years for oil companies to adjust to the deflationary times. It took years to bring costs in line with expenses and for profitability to return. The entire Wall Street community was bearish on oil stocks for much of that period. And they were right.

The actual turning point came a bit later, as Jeff recalls. It was at a research analysts' meeting in New York. An executive for a major oil services company was giving a presentation to Wall Street analysts at the New York Society of Security Analysts. These presentations are standard fare on Wall Street. Company executives attend these near-daily luncheons to describe conditions within their industries and inside their own firms. At this meeting, in the latter half of the 1980s, the executive stood up before the crowd and opened his speech with the following line:

"I can't understand why anybody would buy our stock in this business."

It was the ultimate buy signal, the ultimate sign of capitulation. Even the company's chief executive thought his own business would never improve. Jeff remembers that the stock doubled in the next year. It went up 100% at a time when it seemed all hope was lost. That's how contrarian investing works. And that's how the manager of the nation's biggest mutual fund makes his money.

The Sure Thing

Michael Aronstein is one of Wall Street's deepest thinkers. A Harvard philosophy and history major, he seems an unlikely player in the rough-and-tumble world of Wall Street. He looks a bit professorial in his khaki-colored pants, tweed jacket, and bow tie. But he is as much a student of the markets as he is a teacher, always looking to learn a lesson from the markets. He is humble that way. But he is also firm in his convictions when it comes to the big picture. He makes his bets, unlike traders and stock pickers, through a top-down approach to investing. This approach has served him well over the years.

In a top-down approach, an investor looks at the global economy, assessing the direction of interest rates worldwide, the rate of growth and inflation, and the relative attractiveness of financial assets compared to tangible assets. Once that is put into perspective, the top-down investor makes his choices among all investment opportunities and prays to God he is right.

In the 1980s Michael Aronstein was one-third of a prominent investment firm known as Comstock Partners. Comstock was a group of former Merrill Lynch analysts who decided to strike out on their own in search of a present-day Comstock Lode. It would not be in silver, though, that they made their fortunes, but in U.S. Treasury bonds. At one point in the mid-1980s, Comstock controlled about 2% of all the outstanding thirty-year Treasury bonds in the market. Several billion dollars were in tow. The bonds were purchased because Mike, Stan Salvigsen, and Charlie Minter were certain the U.S. economy, after a buoyant and speculative stretch in the 1980s, was going to deflate. And in a deflationary environment, bonds gain in purchasing power and value.

After much analysis and historical study, they reasoned that the U.S. economy of the 1980s was very much similar to the economy of the 1920s. Money was cheap. Very cheap. So cheap it fueled an economic growth spurt unparalleled in modern times. It produced an inflation that everyone viewed as benign, since the inflation was in real estate prices, stock prices, and bond prices. That's the kind of inflation that few people worry about. The Dow Jones industrial average, for example, vaulted to new all-time highs with serial regularity, particularly in 1986 and 1987. Corporate profits were bulging and individuals were having an economic party, going on a borrowing binge that was nearly without precedent. Property prices skyrocketed in the United States, both in the 1920s and in the 1980s. It was a bubble that just couldn't last. When the bust came, bonds would be the investment of choice, despite the fantastic run they had already seen in 1982. Comstock's big bets on bonds proved quite profitable in the middle 1980s.

The Comstock partners also managed to exit the stock market before the 1987 crash. They were among the hottest hands on Wall Street at that time. That's not to say they've always had the Midas touch. In fact, they suffered a dry spell in the late 1980s and early 1990s.

After some philosophical disagreements on the proper top-down view, Michael Aronstein left the partnership a few years ago and formed West Course Capital, a small investment firm with about $100 million under management. He remains among the most thoughtful players on the Street. Interestingly enough, Aronstein says his best lessons came not from making a ton of money, but from losing some. Fortunately for him, most of those lessons came early in his career, when the stakes weren't quite as high.

Mike Aronstein got an early start investing and trading. After Harvard, he entered the training program at Merrill Lynch. There the philosophy student found religion in the financial markets. Aronstein started his career with an annual salary of $10,000. By the time he graduated the training program, he was raking in all of $12,000 a year. He was given the office of Wyatt Weld, a prominent figure in Merrill's history, and was ready to take Wall Street by storm.

Michael quickly swung into the Wall Street routine. Every morning Merrill Lynch's staff, like countless other brokerage houses, began the day with a conference call. Economists, analysts, and traders offer their assessments of the day's business, forecasting the direction of interest rates, telling the sales force about a hot new stock or making an early call on the expected direction of stock prices. A few months into Mike Aronstein's work life, one of Merrill's technical analysts was making his daily comments on what the charts were saying about individual stocks. Mike recalls the words of the prognosticator as if he heard them last night over cocktails.

"I want to tell you, I see one stock here that looks like the most powerful thing I've ever seen in my entire career."

Mike remembers the hush that came over the office. Brokers and traders love a sure thing. And when someone discovers one, the entire office sits up and takes notice, just like in those old E. F. Hutton commercials. The Merrill employees put their coffee cups down. The analyst began describing the stock.

"It's 44 3/8. It looks like $42 is absolute, cold support (a permanent floor for the price). This thing looks like it won't stop. It looks like a locomotive."

By that day, a twenty-five-year-old Michael Aronstein had saved up a princely sum, for a youngster on a fixed salary. He had, over only a few months time, squirreled away $1,000, six or seven weeks' after-tax pay. He decided to play the stock Merrill's technician recommended. It would be a quick killing.

On the advice of the analyst, he bought call options on Storage Technology, the firm that makes data storage devices for computers. Mike bought Storage Tech, "45 calls." A call option allows an investor the right to buy the underlying stock at a predetermined price by a fixed future date. Call options increase in value as the underlying stock goes up. In this case, each call option contract gave Michael the right to buy 100 shares of Storage Technology at $45 a share by a certain expiration date in the future. To buy them he paid 7/8 of a point each for a hundred contracts. His total bill, with commissions included, was $937. He put down six weeks' salary on a single bet. It was a rather large percentage of his net worth at the time.

Storage Technology never traded at 44 3/8 again. It went down for fifteen years, straight. Mike's option position lasted five weeks before it expired worthless. He lost half his net worth in his first big trade. He never lost that much again.

But he learned what men have known through the millennia. Only two things are certain, death and taxes. He also learned that other old adages became old adages for a reason. If something seems too good to be true, it usually is.

Taxi . . .

Martin Sass has been in the investment business for quite some time, from his days as a "hot stocks" analyst at Argus research back in the 1970s, to running his own firm, M. D. Sass & Co, which now boasts over $2 billion in assets. Sass, a snappy dresser, looks a little like Gordon Gekko, the villain in Oliver Stone's *Wall Street*, but with none of the venom, nor any of the other sundry bad habits associated with movie bad guys. A pleasant chap, generous with his time, Sass has become one of the Street's most successful spotters of undervalued or overvalued stocks.

Since his rather humble beginnings he has become one of the most respected money men on the Street, a frequent guest on business TV, and widely quoted in the financial press. His specialty these days involves buying into distressed companies and turning them back into viable and profitable enterprises. But he earned his reputation as someone to reckon with by doing just the opposite of that—he identified overvalued stocks and told investors to sell. The call that made him famous is a most compelling tale.

Traders' Tales

In the early 1960s, Marty Sass was an enterprising lad. He was fresh out of Brooklyn College where he studied accounting, when he landed his first job on the Street. In 1963 he started at Argus Research, as a junior analyst making $60 a week, not a ton of money for a young go-getter who dreamed of the good life. His high school sweetheart was his new bride, so the young family man had more than one mouth to feed, making him just a little hungry for success.

Flash back, as they say in the entertainment business, to the early 1960s. Television had pretty much become the national pastime, capturing the hearts, minds, and advertising dollars of a thriving postwar generation. While its Golden Age had already passed, TV was still in its infancy in the 1960s, penetrating house after house after house, until the entire nation was wired, not just for sound, but for pictures as well. Black and white pictures, but still live moving images had implanted themselves in nearly every American home.

As TV saturated the nation, the business of selling sets was maturing. And as soon as the old black and whites filled most homes in the country, TV went through another revolution, as color sets made the old black and white TVs immediately obsolete.

Martin Sass was very quickly adept at identifying opportunities. So he asked his superiors at Argus to let him analyze the color TV business, as one of his "beats." Back then, about 3% of American households had color sets: 100% had black and white sets on which they would watch *Bonanza* and the *Ed Sullivan Show*, among other favorites. Sass saw that color sets would quickly become the next growth vehicle in the consumer electronics business. So he followed the companies that would be the vehicles of future growth in the industry. Motorola, RCA, and Zenith were among the native names that dominated the color business back when.

So Sass began to familiarize himself with the business, visiting plants, studying balance sheets, doing the things that financial analysts do. Then he took a fateful trip to Chicago, where he was scheduled to meet the management of Motorola, the company that eventually turned out Quasar sets, so widely touted on TV. He wanted to know how the sets were selling, how much inventory the manufacturers had, any bit of information that would offer a clue about the future earnings potential of a firm such as Motorola.

But it was in the back of a cab, not in the manager's suite, that Martin Sass found out some interesting things about the production of color sets. Sass hailed a cab upon arriving at Chicago's O'Hare airport. It would prove to be the ride of a lifetime. As it just so happened, the cab driver was a laid-off Motorola production worker. The cabbie had been idled because Motorola overproduced a large batch of color TV sets, for which there were few buyers at the time. The color TV business, like its black and white brother before it, had begun to saturate its market, a factor that leads to an inevitable slow down in sales, even in a budding business. The cabbie's story was a warning to Marty that the high-flying color TV companies were in for a pounding on Wall Street, if the news about a slowdown got out.

He thanked the cabbie for the ride and stepped out to meet with Motorola management. As he remembers the meeting, the managers downplayed the notion of excess production, and the bulging inventories of unwanted sets.

(Temporarily unwanted, to be sure, but enough to alter earnings expectations for the companies involved.) After meeting with management, Marty was left dissatisfied with their answers to his probing questions. He decided to confirm his worst suspicions about the impending fate of the color TV industry.

Marty figured a local bar was as good a place to start as any other native institution. If the cabbie's story were true, then surely other idled workers would be frittering away time. At the watering hole, several other out-of-work laborers confirmed the cab driver's story. Motorola had piled up huge inventories of color sets, which were not selling as quickly as expected. Sass sensed that the glory days of the domestic color TV set business were quickly coming to an end. Indeed, it would not be long after these days that Japanese rivals began outselling U.S. firms in the color set business and even acquiring the remains of what had been a thriving domestic television production industry.

Sass hopped a plane back to Wall Street and issued a "sell" recommendation on the entire TV group, a brash call that was refuted in a press release from Motorola. But the press release couldn't stop sellers from selling. And sell they did. TV stocks collapsed. Marty Sass found his fame on the Street.

[Motorola today remains a vibrant company, making semiconductors and cellular phones. It no longer produces television sets. In fact, not a single company that made sets in the United States still does so today. RCA was acquired by General Electric in 1985. Its color TV business was sold by GE to the French firm, Thomson, S.A. Zenith Electronics, the last firm to make TVs domestically, shifting all its production offshore.]

Leon Cooperman

There are all different types of players on Wall Street. There are brokers, traders, speculators, and investors. Brokers take orders from customers. Traders dart in and out of the market, scalping eighths and quarters countless times a day. They profit from short-term swings in the markets. Investors, for the most part, buy and hold their investments for longer periods of time. They make large commitments that, over the long run, will provide satisfactory returns. And then there are hedge fund speculators. They do everything from making short-term trades that capture small profits, to making big bets that can result in spectacular gains or sizable losses.

Leon Cooperman has been both a long-term investor and a hedge fund speculator. He had phenomenal success as an investment strategist, but lately, he's been living the life of a speculator. On Wall Street, as in the wild, it is difficult for a leopard to change its spots. Leon Cooperman has been finding that out of late.

Cooperman believes that each person has a certain number of great ideas in his or her lifetime. The key to success, then, is to know when those opportunities present themselves and to then play them in a large way.

For many years, Leon Cooperman was the chief market strategist of the prestigious Wall Street firm, Goldman Sachs & Co. Since then, he has formed his own hedge fund,

Omega Advisors, a firm that plays in many markets all at once. From individual stocks to international bonds to foreign currencies, Omega is among the elite, independent firms known as hedge funds. Its track record has been solid in the 1990s. Despite some difficult times, particularly in 1994, Leon Cooperman remains among the most highly regarded players in the investment game, up 113% since founding Omega in 1992.

Leon admits that his best bets have been made in the long-term arena, as an investor. A good investor can profit handsomely from a single, bright idea. A trader or speculator, on the other hand, has to act on several ideas, oftentimes simultaneously, to keep the profits rolling in. Buy, sell, buy, sell. The actions of a trader are hair-trigger and often capitalize on minute discrepancies in the prices of securities. With luck, their cumulative capitalizing adds up to big bucks. But it's different for an investor, one home run over the long haul can produce enough money on which to retire. Leon Cooperman hit a few home runs early in his career.

Back in 1972 shares of Lin Broadcasting, an owner of television stations, media businesses, and cellular telephone licenses, was trading near $15. The brainchild of Don Dels, Lin was getting a reputation as an up-and-coming communications company, with attractive growth prospects and an equally attractive stock price. However, 1972 proved to be the beginning of a rough row to hoe for stock market investors. The economy of the 1970s was not favorable for financial assets. Nor was the political climate in the good ol' U.S.A. The Vietnam War was still raging, Watergate was just starting to tear at the fabric of America. And inflation was about to burst on the scene, a deadly combination of influences that made stocks relatively unattractive in coming years.

Starting in 1972 Lin Broadcasting shares nosedived, falling all the way to about $2 1/8 per share in November of 1974. The great bear market of 1973–74 ravaged small stocks on Wall Street, as well as most of the big ones. The environment for buying stocks was so poor that many analysts on Wall Street feared the worst—that the economy, the markets, and individual companies would head into an inexorable slide from which there was little hope for return.

By 1974, an oil crisis, a wage-price spiral, and a general sense of malaise began to grip the country as the economy lurched from inflation to recession. As a result, President Gerald Ford and his chief economic advisor, Alan Greenspan, decided to "Whip Inflation Now!" (WIN). That optimistic economic policy was a dismal failure. And in the post-Watergate era, little hope remained for improvement, either in the economy or in the national psyche. The stock market cratered in 1974.

But as is always the case, too much pessimism on both Main Street and Wall Street can often be a sign that the tide is about to turn. That's when Leon Cooperman decided to take a flyer on Lin Broadcasting. Remember that Lin, despite bullish prognostications back in 1972, had gone from $15 a share to just over $2 a share by November of 1974. At this point Leon Cooperman had one of his best ideas ever.

Leon visited a good friend, an analyst inside Goldman Sachs who followed Lin for the firm. The analyst thought the company still had solid prospects and a potentially lucrative future, if only the overall tide would turn. With that Leon Cooperman promptly walked over to Goldman's trading desk and purchased 5,000 shared of Lin. The entire investment cost $12,000. Meantime, the economy and market environment improved. It would be nearly eight years before the economy would explode in the Reagan boom years, but Leon Cooperman remained patient and allowed his $12,000 investment to grow.

And grow it did. Lin went on to become a pioneer company in the telephone and cellular businesses, snapping up wireless communications licenses and parlaying its skill in that area into a quite valuable franchise. Leon used his profits from Lin to finance his charitable contributions. Leon's lone lament is that he should have given away cash and kept his Lin shares. Had he kept them, he would have seen four splits, and his holdings grow to 80,000 shares. His investment would have been worth $12 million because Lin was ultimately bought by AT&T for $150 a share! Sometimes charity should start at home.

Short Takes

You've already met money manager, Ron Baron, of Baron Capital. Baron, a widely regarded investor manages about $500 million these days. He looks for strong growth-oriented companies whose stocks will rise faster than the general market, providing above average rates of return for himself and his investors. He likes to buy stocks that he thinks will double over a few years time. Everyone would. But that's his stated goal, and he sticks by it.

In years past, however, Baron also liked to go the other way—to short stocks for the long run. Traders who engage in short selling borrow securities from their broker, and sell at the prevailing market price. They are betting (and hoping) that the stock goes down. If and when it does, they buy it back at the cheaper price and pocket the difference. It's the inverse of buying. It's a style of investing that requires a unique talent and, sometimes, a taste for the negative. Many famous traders and investors have taken the plunge on the short side and profited handsomely over the years.

In Ron's early career, shorting stocks was among his favorite pastimes. He looked for stocks that were wildly overvalued, based on their fundamental prospects: companies whose stock prices reflected too rosy a profit outlook, stocks that were vulnerable to disappointment. Ron also liked to look for out-and-out frauds, knowing that the stocks of fraudulent concerns would ultimately collapse, if and when the truth about their operations ever leaked out.

Ron Baron made some serious money identifying both.

A Dog with Fleas

Hartz Mountain, the flea collar company, was among the first short sales Ron Baron made. The company grew into a household name in the 1970s, selling flea collars and doggie toys to a nation of pet owners. Their product lines expanded over time as they catered to all sorts of pets, from dogs to cats to birds. When the company's business started to tire, like an old hound after a hunt, Ron Baron sang his song to Wall Street, just like a canary.

Baron recalls that Hartz Mountain stock came public at around $18 a share and quickly skyrocketed, nearly doubling in a few short months. But, unlike many others, he was not enamored with the company's prospects after poring over the company's books. Baron felt, at the time, that Hartz Mountain was, itself, a dog with fleas. The company was getting 20% of its sales from dog collars, which was fine. But the collars accounted for 30% of the profits, which meant Hartz was far too reliant on one product for its good fortune. Sensing some other canine characteristics, Baron sold the stock short in the low thirties, nearly double its initial public offering price. He recommended other traders and investors do the same. The stock quickly began a descent that troubled Hartz executives, who had been to the mountain of high stock prices and were not willing to come down.

Baron's tactics angered the owner of Hartz Mountain, Leonard Stern. When Stern visited Baron's office, Ron recalls a screaming match that ended with Stern banging his shoe on Baron's desk in an outburst reminiscent of Nikita Kruschev's United Nations tirade. While Kruschev threatened to bury his archenemy, the United States, Stern was a bit more diplomatic. He threatened to sue. But in the end Stern's threats proved as empty as Kruschev's. And Ron Baron prevailed.

Hartz Mountain shares, despite Stern's contention that Baron was wrong, plummeted, falling as low as $8 a share. The stock was mauled by a deteriorating profit performance. Vindicated, Baron bought his short position back at around $8, making better than $22 a share in profits.

While Leonard Stern was angry, he was not a fool. In time, he bought the company back from public shareholders at $12 a share. He repurchased the company on the cheap, in some ways, with a little help from Ron Baron.

Shortly after Stern took the company private, Baron decided to give him a ring. This, as they say in the business, took some balls on Baron's part.

"Leonard, you know, you were able to do a great deal because of me. I'm calling you to say that you've got a lot of money and you need someone to manage it. Why don't you have me manage some money for you?"

"Are you crazy?" Stern shouted, somewhat shocked that the man he held responsible for driving down his stock, would call looking to generate business for himself.

That bridge had been burned. Baron and Stern never talked again.

Doctor, Doctor, It Hurts When I Do That

Another one of Ron Baron's fondest short-selling memories involves an outwardly fraudulent firm, American Surgery Centers (ASC). It was a stock that made more than a few investors ill. It was a company that poisoned the well of capitalism, if only for a brief moment in the history of the market.

Baron recalls a calm day in 1983, at the height of the speculative run in small stocks. Back then, investors were engaging in a feeding frenzy on Wall Street, buying any little stock that was sold to the public. High technology firms, medical companies, and even companies that made video games were all the rage.

Ron Baron was at work when a knock on the door stirred him from his daily routine. A heavy man and a buxom blonde with all the charm of a 42nd Street hooker walked into his office, ready to pitch Baron on the investment of a lifetime—American Surgery Centers. The heavy-set entrepreneur, charming as a longshoreman with a labor complaint, ran outpatient surgery centers that were fast replacing emergency rooms as the treatment center of choice. He owned four or five centers, as Ron recalls, each losing a substantial sum of money.

But that didn't prevent American Surgery Center's stock from climbing. In the small stock mania of 1983, ASC jumped from 50 cents a share to $2.50, in a matter of months. Investors, at the time, cared little for reality in this speculative mania and bought ASC because the company's concept was new and exciting.

The pudgy entrepreneur wanted Baron to invest in the company and take some stock off his hands for $2.50 a share. Baron, never having met the man before, was a bit intrigued and asked the man to send him some financial reports.

Baron pored over the firm's books, analyzing the firm's business prospects and its profit and loss statement. In short, he reviewed every last stitch of this surgical operation. After a thorough examination, Ron found out that the only way the centers showed any profit at all, was through the sale of stock to the public. The surgical centers themselves never reached the critical mass required to make any money. Instead, the company stayed afloat by selling stock to a public with an insatiable appetite for small, hot stocks. The proceeds of the stock sales, Ron recalls, paid the company's operating expenses. They lost money on treating patients. That was not a healthy way to do business.

Cut to six months later. Small stocks are still the rage on Wall Street. Investors are buying any hot little stock they can get their hot little hands on. The small cap stock market was boiling. It was a market that defied logic and was ultimately doomed to crash. About that time, Ron Baron remembers a night out with his wife and kids. He was sitting at the bar of a local restaurant when he overheard a most interesting conversation.

Sitting beside him at the bar were two young men, likely in their mid-twenties, discussing the stock market. Always interested, Ron listened to the youngsters brag about their recent stock market successes. In some ways, the scene was reminiscent of the old E. F. Hutton commercial, where at the very end of the ad the client says, "Well, my broker is E. F. Hutton. And E. F. Hutton says. . . ." Of course, everyone in the place stops what they're doing to hear what E. F. Hutton is saying. The scene repeated itself with Ron. As the two youngsters chatted, one said "My broker is the best I've ever seen. He's never done anything wrong."

The other chap asked, "What's your broker buying now?"

And the proud lad responded, "My broker is buying American Surgical Centers. Thinks it's going to $17 in two months." Imagine, $17! Remember that the last time Ron Baron even thought about the stock, it was trading at $2.50 a share.

After dining with his wife and kids, Ron raced home. He left his family at the door and rushed to the office. Bear in mind that Baron had not so much as punched up ASC's stock price once in the six months since the surgery center's owner had come in. When he called up the stock price on his Quotron machine, American Surgery was trading at $12 a share, up from $2.50 a few short months before. After reexamining the company's prospects, he decided to short the stock. He told his clients to short the stock. After a quick recheck on the firm, Ron found that the company had the same problems then as it did six months earlier. It was still losing money on each surgery center and still buoying its balance sheet by selling stock. Oh yes, it was also telling investors that it planned to expand its operations overseas. It touted the fact that it was set to open centers throughout Saudi Arabia and Europe.

Ultimately, none of the promises proved true. Nonetheless the stock rallied after Baron shorted it. It rose all the way to $19 a share. But Ron kept shorting the stock despite the pain of losing money on each sale. Short sellers lose money selling a stock when the stock goes up, the same way a buyer loses money when a stock goes down. The only difference is that on the downside, a stock can only fall to zero. If he buys a stock at $10 and it goes to zero, he loses $10 a share. But a short-seller can lose more than everything. If he shorts a stock at $10 and it goes to $100 and he hasn't cancelled his trade, he's out $90 a share! That's why short selling can be a most dangerous game to play.

Fortunately, for Ron, *Barron's*, the weekly financial magazine, panned the stock based on Ron's analysis. The stock promptly collapsed, like one of American Surgical's own patients. It fell back to $12 and Ron made some money. Ultimately he rode the stock to zero. American Surgery Centers got sicker, then died.

A few short takes from a man who, today, only goes long.

Investment Biker

Jimmy Rogers will be the first to tell you that he's the world's worst trader. He's made a lot of money from investing but trading is not his strong suit. Not that he hasn't done it—it's just that he doesn't think he does it well. Jimmy Rogers, "the investment biker," has earned a phenomenal living from investing, but some of his trading tales are quite telling. Jimmy's early mistakes taught him that markets do not always do what you expect when you expect it. He's learned that you can be right about the direction of a market but wrong about the timing of the

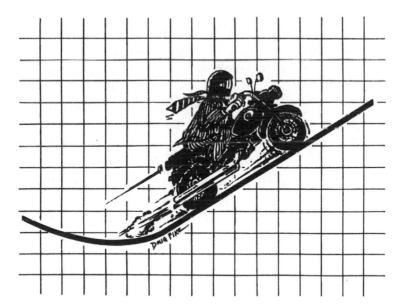

INVESTMENT BIKER

move. He also learned, quite early, that unless you have sufficient capital, being right only counts if you're right at the right time. Today, Jimmy is an investor, not a trader. Luckily, an investor can be right at the wrong time if he has patience. A trader who's right at the wrong time, however, isn't a trader for very long.

Jimmy Rogers lives in a multistory Manhattan house, lavishly decorated and generously populated with art works and artifacts from his many travels. He has dark hair and a quick smile. Equally quick is his thinking, which allows him to calculate the risks and rewards of every situation he's in and usually profit from the moment. In physical stature, he is not a tall man, although he stands head and shoulders above most of his peers, when it comes to his business. His lilting Southern drawl evokes a slightly "down home" feeling about Jimmy, but he has been anything but down home for much of his life. Author of *Investment Biker*, an epic work that chronicles his two-year motorcycle trip around the globe, Jimmy has traveled the world over, scouring the planet for new and exciting investment opportunities. From Sao Paulo to Siberia, from New York to New Zealand, Jimmy's well-documented journey took him to exotic locales in search of undiscovered profits. He has been living the good life that only a few investors can enjoy.

Jimmy sprang from humble beginnings in Alabama, but ultimately prospered in a world that humbles more of its participants than it rewards. Today Jimmy is a wealthy private investor and an occasional finance professor at Columbia University. He got his start with another legend of Wall Street: George Soros. Together they made millions with the Quantum Fund, the investment fund that Soros still runs today. Jimmy, for his part took the money and ran, choosing not to live his life tied every moment to the computer screen. As Jimmy will tell you, he moved on to other equally exciting adventures.

One of Jimmy's earliest experiences in the stock market was both exalting and humbling. He recalls the stock market of 1970, a year that ushered in a crushing bear market, wiping out the gilded go-go era of the late 1960s, when mutual fund investing was all the rage. Jimmy hadn't been at the stock market game more than two years at that time. But he knew a troubled stock market when he saw one. So he took all the money he had and bought put options on the stock market.

Jimmy tripled his stake in five months. By May of 1970 the stock market had suffered its worst decline since the bone-crushing bear market of 1937. As Jimmy recalls, he sold out his winning trade on the very day the market touched bottom. He'd made a killing all the while his peers were getting killed in the market.

All around Wall Street, Jimmy felt the ire of those who were suddenly suffering. The bear market of 1970 brought down old-line Wall Street firms and cost countless men their richly rewarding jobs as the go-go era passed even more quickly than it came. From this experience Jimmy learned to keep a low profile. In reality, he didn't profit from anyone's misfortune. But in life, perception is everything. To others around him, Jimmy sensed they resented his profiting while they did poorly. He learned then and there never to boast of his market successes.

Jimmy was emboldened by his early score, thinking, "This is easy. I'm going to be the next Bernard Baruch. I'm going to be rich."

At that point, Jimmy decided he would tackle the market again, hoping to catch the next decline in prices with equal skill. But even as a young trader, Jimmy knew that no market travels in a straight line. There would be an inevitable bear market rally, just to confound all those who were sure the market had nowhere to go but down. And rally the market did, rising sharply through June and July of 1970. But Jimmy felt the rise was nothing more than a "dead cat bounce," as they call it on Wall Street. So he decided to plunge into the market once again. But instead of buying puts, which allow traders to profit from the downside with quite limited risk, Jimmy opted to really make a killing when the bear lumbered back on to Wall Street. He decided to sell short a basket of individual stocks. By selling the borrowed securities and hoping to buy them back at lower prices, Jimmy could clip the difference and make another killing. He thought it would be an easy way to duplicate his early success in plunging the market. Plus it was potentially far more rewarding.

But it was not without risk. Once a stock is shorted, should it go up, the seller has unlimited vulnerability. If one shorts a stock at 50 and it goes to 40, one makes $10 a share from the downside move. If it goes to zero, $50 is the profit. But what happens if it goes to $60, $80, or $100 or even higher? The losses don't stop until the stock stops going up. It's the riskiest strategy on Wall Street. (At least it was back then.) Jimmy found out the hard way that the game isn't always as simple as it seems.

Unfortunately for Jim Rogers, the market didn't stop going up at the end of July or early August, as he prophesied. It kept going higher into the autumn, and so did all the stocks he shorted. By September, he was wiped out! Ironically, Jimmy was proved right about his stocks' long-term direction. After he was wiped out, those shares eventually promptly plunged again. But it was too late for Jimmy, being too early in the market meant being out of cash—for the time being. As in comedy, Jimmy learned a key lesson about trading—timing is everything!

Rogers has an expression that he always impresses upon novice investors. He frequently admonishes them to "do their homework!" The phrase may stem from Jimmy's professorial leanings or from some hard-learned lessons that taught him the value of research. Whatever the origins, homework is now the central theme in Jimmy's investment strategies.

Jimmy learned about doing his homework from University Computing (UC), a high-flying stock that was one of the big winners on Wall Street in the late 1960s. At the time Jimmy hated the market and hated this stock. So he decided to sell it short. He was not enamored of the company's prospects, nor did he like the prospects for the stock market in early 1970. In the first phase of that 1970 bear market, University Computing had fallen from 180 to 40. Jimmy felt it was a lead-pipe cinch that the stock would fall still further. But like the rest of the market, Jimmy knew UC was due for a bounce.

After a brief bounce, he decided to begin his experiment in short selling by shorting University when it climbed back to $50. Rogers was sure that University Computing had seen its best days, and that even at its current discounted prices it was a candidate for sale. In fact, Jimmy's research told him it was a $2 stock. So, as we said, he shorted the stock at $50. Ultimately it went to $2. But it went to $96 first. Bounced from $40 to $96 on its way to $2. It was Jimmy's worst trade ever.

After his early successes and failures, Jimmy studied the markets and studied individual stocks, making sure he knew not just the fundamentals of the investments he planned to make, but how to time his moves with greater precision. That is not to say that Jimmy Rogers has been right about all markets at all times. No one ever is. But, he is an astute student of finance, from balance sheet analysis to understanding the details of a variety of businesses.

Among the most important lessons Jimmy ever learned was that for traders and investors, knowledge is power. But the knowledge needed to trade or invest can never be incomplete. A little knowledge in the exacting business of the markets can be a dangerous thing, as Jimmy Rogers found out again, later, in the 1970s, as the next story shows.

Plumbing the Depths

After World War II, indoor plumbing became a standard feature in newly constructed homes across America. It had not necessarily been a uniform feature of home building before the age of mass-produced housing. But the explosion of Levittowns and the rise of suburbia gave way to home building that included all the amenities necessary for a comfortable, modern life. And while homes across the country had included indoor plumbing for several decades, the standard features we have come to expect in the kitchens and bathrooms today were hardly standard before planned communities sprang up everywhere around the nation.

In the early days of indoor plumbing, sinks generally had two faucets, one for hot and one for cold water. It was quite common to scald one's hands under the hot water faucet or chill them unnecessarily under the cold. But American ingenuity remedied that. Masco Corporation's founders invented the single-faucet sink. In a single stroke of genius, the founder of the company built a thriving, profitable business from a reasonably low-technology innovation.

But by the 1970s Jimmy Rogers was sufficiently convinced that Masco's single-faucet business was peaking. The market for selling new faucets or replacing the older, double-faucet models was maturing. Other firms, which sensed a profit opportunity in the single-faucet industry, were entering the business and undercutting Masco's prices. Another trend that Jimmy spotted involved the changing demographics of the business. Household formation was taking a breather after a breakneck pace in the postwar years. The baby boomers had set up house and had established their permanent places in the new economy. Home construction and family formation peaked together in the 1970s as the boomers settled into their quiet family lives in their newly acquired homes.

In fact, new housing construction, in absolute terms, saw its highest levels in U.S. history in the early 1970s. It has not been as strong in any economic recovery period since. In both the 1980s and 1990s, new home construction has fallen short of the lofty levels reached back then. For Jimmy, then, there were enough signs to suggest that Masco's stock should decline, since its best years were most likely behind it. The company had acknowledged that fact by going on an acquisition binge, buying other, faster growing businesses that might pick up the slack. Jimmy Rogers believed that the acquisition binge was a bald admission by management that the faucet business wasn't going to be the cash cow it once was. If it was still hot, Jimmy reasoned, there would be no reason for the company to diversify.

On top of all that, Masco's stock price was expensive. The company's stock sold at a huge multiple of its expected earnings, sporting what Wall Streeters call a "lofty price/earnings ratio," a key measure of stock valuation that suggested the stock was pricey by historic standards. So, Jimmy decided to sell Masco short. He dumped the stock and waited for the faucet-maker's stock to sink.

At the same time Jimmy grew disenchanted with the single-faucet business, he found an industry of which he was quite enamored. The CB radio business. Citizens band (CB) radios are the communications devices that truckers often use to talk to one another on their long and lonely journeys over the highways and byways of the country. For some unknown reason, the culture of the trucking community captured the nation's hearts and minds in the mid-1970s, leading to a most embarrassing period in U.S. cultural history when nearly everyone in the country strove to imitate eighteen-wheel truck drivers. The business had a language all its own, which many people adopted as their own, if only briefly.

"Breaker, breaker, good buddy. This is the love bandit. I got a smokey on my tail and a fifth in my lap. I'm putting the hammer down and clearing out. Catch you on the fly. Ten-four. Good buddy, I'm out."

The CB craze spawned everything from popular songs about trucking to the Smokey and the Bandit action flicks. It was the period just preceding disco and just following dinosaur rock. But fortunately for true culture vultures it was a blue-collar diversion that disappeared as fast as it takes an eighteen-wheeler to roll out of town. Nonetheless, sales of CB radios exploded in the early and mid-1970s, creating a nation of good buddies who touched each other's lives every time they went on the road again. Jimmy Rogers scored big with his CB investments, buying shares of E. F. Johnson, a CB radio company, whose sales and profits exploded during those days. Meantime, though, Jimmy's CB profits were hurt by that short sale of Masco. The stock never dropped as Jimmy had expected it to. The stock's performance fooled Jimmy because, as Jimmy admits, he didn't do his homework.

Rogers thought Masco made a big mistake by making a host of acquisitions. The firm financed the purchases of unrelated companies by borrowing large sums of money, an unattractive way to buy businesses. However, one of those acquisitions turned out to be a company that made police radio scanners. Now if you're old enough, you'll remember that these one-way communications devices were also quite popular during the CB craze. Nosy Americans listened in to police conversations and emergency calls, snooping for local tragedies they could go witness when the TV shows of the time were too boring to watch.

Unfortunately for Jimmy, sales at Masco's newly acquired scanner company jumped from about $3 million to over $100 million in a short time. The soaring sales helped Masco's bottom line immediately, keeping the company in the black and Jimmy Rogers in the red. So, Masco's stock went up, not down. Jimmy's short sale went south.

Ironically, Jimmy knew the fundamentals of both the CB business and the single-faucet business quite well. He never imagined that the company he sold short would buy into the business that he liked so very much. He simply didn't do his homework thoroughly enough to keep himself from losing money. He ignored the fact that Masco bought a company in an industry that he, himself, was buying into.

That's why Jimmy Rogers always says, "Do your homework!"

Crash Tales

The 1987 stock market crash was a watershed event in modern financial history. Although it was not as devastating a blow to Main Street as the crash of 1929, it dealt a crushing blow to Wall Street. The crash was a closing chapter in the Roaring 80s, a meltdown that reminded investment professionals just how vulnerable they are to an abrupt reversal of fortune.

The 1987 crash was also noteworthy because it illustrated quite clearly the new ways in which world markets operated. The creation of sophisticated new investment products, the impact of technological innovation and the new-found ability to speed money around the globe in a millisecond all played a part in the market meltdown that gripped Wall Street nearly a decade ago.

The crash also taught individual investors a new lesson—that it's always okay to "buy the dip." Indeed, since the crash of '87, investors have been amply rewarded for increasing their stock holdings every time the market declines. It is a lesson that many hope will not prove disastrous the next time the market swoons.

The following tales are some little-known stories about the wild events that occurred during and around that fateful day in October. There are a few lessons here, plus some tales meant to surprise and amuse.

Crash Specialist

From the perspective of a New York Stock Exchange specialist, the 1987 stock market crash was an unbelievable event. Specialists match buyers and sellers of various stocks. They control the so-called auction system on the exchange, which allows stocks to be bought or sold on the floor. They tell buyers the price at which a seller is willing to sell and tell sellers the price at which a buyer is willing to buy. Often, the buyers and sellers split the difference.

In addition to functioning as auctioneer, the specialist is also charged with maintaining orderly and fair markets in the 2,500 or so stocks on the Big Board. If, for instance there are no buyers for a particular stock, but there is a seller, the specialist may have to buy the stock himself. He can resell it at a later date, provided buyers reemerge. In short, a specialist must sell stocks to buyers when there are no sellers and buy stocks from sellers when there are no buyers. All of their actions are taken to ensure the market for stocks is liquid and efficient.

Everyday their firm's capital is at risk. On any given day, a specialist's shop could shut down because of some unforeseen market event or some incredibly unfortunate trading mistake. That is not to say the job of the specialist is without its rewards—the age-old job of making markets in stocks is a hugely profitable enterprise.

Still there are days when the very fabric of a specialist's life might be torn apart.

Bob Scavone knows those days quite well. He has worked on the Big Board floor since 1948. He has seen the market respond to an assortment of unforeseen events; Truman's unexpected victory in the 1946 presidential race, Eisenhower's heart attack, the missiles of October, the death of Kennedy, the Vietnam War, the Hunt brothers' silver scandal and, of course, the crash of '87. Despite bearing witness to a host of tragedies that have affected both the nation and the stock market, Scavone is also well known for his sense of humor, particularly the gallows-type humor that Wall Street is best known for in rather tragic circumstances.

October 19, 1987, was a particularly trying and tiring day for investors and traders. But the specialist community on the floor of the Big Board was hit unexpectedly hard. Specialists spent the entire day buying stock from panicked sellers, at increasingly lower prices. They bought the stock with no guarantee that prices would rebound in the foreseeable future. Had the market collapsed into a full-blown, 1920s-style panic, few specialist firms would have survived the week. But they bought stocks because no one else would and because it was their job. At the end of Black Monday there were few specialists who knew if they'd be in business by the next morning.

Scavone, in his gravelly voice recalls a tumultuousness he had never seen before on Wall Street. The action was so intense that a half day passed before he even bothered to notice the time, thinking only a few minutes had passed since the start of the day. But in the midst of the deluge on Black Monday, Bob Scavone managed to break away for a few moments just after midday. He went outside for a breath of fresh air. The cool street air helped rejuvenate him enough to bring out his famous sense of humor.

Upon stepping outside, Scavone was immediately confronted by reporters, all looking to capture the story of the day. One reporter asked Scavone what was going on inside the Exchange. Scavone described the bedlam in the market.

"People are losing millions. Guys who have built their businesses on the floor for the last forty years are getting wrecked. People are probably going out of business in there." But, the system itself was working, Scavone pointed out to the scoop-hungry reporter.

"The specialists are doing what they are required to do. The teamwork is incredible. Everyone is standing in, doing his job, making the market work."

"How much money is being lost?"

"Millions, billions. Specialists who have spent thirty years earning a reputation are done for. Thirty years of work, gone."

The inquiring mind asked, "Are you a specialist?"

"Yes, I'm a specialist."

The reporter pressed on for more salacious bits of crash-related news.

"Has anyone killed himself? Has anyone jumped out a window?" the reporter asked, salivating at the possibility of getting a scoop. (In the last crash of 1929, Wall Street was thought to be rife with window jumpers.)

"What's happening to you, to your firm? Are you losing money?" the reporter pressed on.

Scavone sullenly replied, "Thirty years, down the drain in three hours."

"What do you do in a case like this?"

Scavone, all seriousness, said, "I called up my wife and said, 'Kaye, fire one of our lifeguards!' "

Scavone then headed back in to trade.

Timing Is Everything

Once in a great while the trading gods look down upon a young trader and smile. Most of the time, though, they favor their chosen, established representatives on earth, like George Soros, Michael Steinhardt, or Julian Robertson. Still, about once in a generation, a young, unknown has greatness thrust upon him, even if it is for just a brief and shining moment. If only for one big, brilliant, and beautiful trade.

Such is the tale of Marty Martino.* Marty is thirty-eight years old and has the reminiscences of a major stock operator. But his fifteen minutes of fame are packed into only a few short months. A few short months that left him a multimillionaire.

You see, Marty made millions upon millions of dollars in the stock market crash of 1987. At only thirty-one years of age, he made the bet of a lifetime, a bet that allowed him a lifetime of leisure. It was a trade that allowed him to walk away from Wall Street before he burned out from the stress and strain of trading the market. That same trade allowed his mother, a struggling schoolteacher, to retire and enjoy her golden years with a golden parachute. His sister, his clients, and his firm all benefited from that one insightful move. A single but keen observation and a single but extremely bold action has secured Marty's place in the trader's Hall of Fame.

Despite the suddenness of his trading success, Marty's one spectacular trade was a trade that he had trained for.

---

*Marty Martino is a real person. His name was changed at his request to protect him and his family from unwanted publicity.

From his first day in the options department of Smith Barney to his last day as a derivatives expert at Morgan Stanley, Marty was born to make one, gargantuan, killer trade.

Marty Martino began his career on Wall Street straight out of college. After a summer job at Smith Barney, learning at the heels of Gil Kemp, Marty Martino was hooked on the markets. So hooked that he wrote his college thesis about stock options and how they work. It was a thesis that would, ultimately more than pay off his college loans, and any other bills he may have had.

Both Marty and the market for equity options were in their professional infancies in the early 1980s. Stock index options had only been introduced to equity investors a few scant years before. Their uses as hedging tools and speculative vehicles were still barely understood, allowing Marty as a novice options specialist to get in on the ground floor of what would be a booming business in derivatives.

As you've seen by now, stock options and stock index options are basically plain vanilla derivatives that allow traders or investors the right to buy or sell a stock or a stock index at a preset price at a future date. The options allow some players to hedge their exposure to stocks or allow others to speculate in equitylike investments at a fraction of the cost of actually buying the underlying securities. Like any derivative instrument, the prices of options track the prices of the underlying investments and can be used as proxies for individual stocks or as proxies for an entire basket of stocks.

But the price of options also takes into account other factors that aren't wholly related to the price of the underlying equity. The volatility of the equity, the general level of interest rates, and the time value of money are important factors in the options equation. This is not pointed out to complicate Marty's story, but to illustrate how complicated options pricing and options trading strategies can be.

Option prices are determined by a complex mathematical equation invented by two college professors who actually understood this stuff. The Black, Scholes model (named for the two professors) allows traders to calculate fair prices for options. Options traders make money when they identify price discrepancies in the options market and capitalize on the momentary abnormalities in the prices of options and the underlying investments. Professors Black and Scholes understood these theories and helped create a national market for stock-related options. This type of intellectuality probably kept them from being invited to more cocktail parties.

Heady stuff, no doubt. But Marty Martino mastered this complicated math on his way to becoming a millionaire. So, after a few stints at medium-size firms, learning the options business from the ground up, in 1981 Marty landed at one of Wall Street's premier firms—Morgan Stanley. He joined its fledgling derivatives unit and began, in earnest, to study the arcane world of options, futures, and other "synthetic" instruments. By 1987 he was ready to make his fame and fortunes on Wall Street.

In the meantime a firm called Leland, O'Brien and Rubenstein was busy making its mark on Wall Street, selling a concept known to investors as "dynamic hedging." It later was popularly called portfolio insurance, a complicated hedging strategy for money managers that has a significant impact on the way Wall Street worked. To put it simply, portfolio insurance was a strategy that allowed equity investors to protect their stock portfolios from unexpected downturns in the equity market. Money managers were taught to sell large amounts of stock index options, or stock index futures, against their equity holdings to profit from a decline in the stock market. Essentially, money managers were selling short the options or futures, while holding onto their entire portfolio of stocks. The futures were used as a proxy for their investments. As the money managers "shorted" the derivative contracts, they would make money from the ongoing decline in stock prices, offsetting the losses in their real portfolios. In this way their exposure to a bear market in stocks was "dynamically hedged." Portfolio insurance was a "black box" program that told the investors to keep selling futures or options until the market stopped going down.

The problem that no one anticipated was that the dumping of those derivative contracts exacerbated market declines, making every act of portfolio insurance selling trigger yet another round of sales. It was a vicious cycle that had disastrous consequences on October 19, 1987.

From his perch in Morgan Stanley's options division, Marty Martino came to realize that hedges weren't actually hedges at all. In fact if everyone tried to hedge their stock portfolios at the same time, he reasoned, the result would be chaos. That chaos would ultimately force the underlying stock market to simply melt down, as all investors rushed to sell simultaneously. It was a thesis that few of the inventors of portfolio insurance ever took seriously. The "rocket scientists" argued that there would never be a series of events that would force all investors to engage in their portfolio protection programs in tandem. Such a scenario would have to precipitate a crash in the market. And a crash simply wasn't on their radar screen.

Crash Tales

Admittedly such rushes to the exit door on Wall Street have been rare occurrences, indeed. There were panics in the past: 1871, 1914, 1921, 1929, 1937, 1969, 1973, 1978, and 1979 all represented market manias that came to an end with a resounding crash on Wall Street. But true market meltdowns were generation events, and, no one in 1987 believed they were part of a "crash generation."

In fact stocks were too busy going up in 1987 for anyone—even the most seasoned of professionals—to worry about a decline. In the first six months of 1987 alone the Dow Jones industrials climbed an eye-popping 27%, a gain almost unprecedented in the annals of market history. It seemed, to borrow a phrase from the 1920s, that the market had reached a "permanent plateau of prosperity." (The noted Yale economist, Irving Fisher, uttered that description of the U.S. economy in 1929, exactly one week before the stock market crash ushered in the Great Depression.)

Hearing ghosts from the past, Marty intuitively understood that the herdlike mentality of investors that dominated the 1980s might just cause as great a selling panic as it did in 1929. Unlike the herd of bulls around him, Marty was intuitive enough to draw parallels to that other time in history when a bull market and unforeseen circumstances combined to crush the wave of economic euphoria that had gripped the nation.

As he compared the "pictures" of the market in 1929 to the market in 1987, he found out that Wall Street was tracing out the exact same pattern that investors followed sixty years before. As he overlaid the two charts, he saw the markets moving in lockstep through the corresponding periods of the year. The only pattern not yet completed in the 1987 chart was the precipitous drop that destroyed the market in 1929. Marty believed that if history was any guide, the coming crash would be the most crushing blow Wall Street had felt in decades. The decline, he reasoned, would also be precipitated by the stunning rise in U.S. interest rates that began in April 1987.

Traders like Marty Martino are men of action. He was armed with the fervent belief that Wall Street, for whatever reasons, was hell-bent on repeating history with frightening exactitude. It would be not just a crash, like the one before, but it would be a crash that was amplified by the modern and menacing mechanics of computerized, black box forces. Those forces would release a selling fury on Wall Street that would make the crash of '29 look like a walk in the park. So Marty decided to make the trade of a lifetime.

In October of 1987, Marty began to make large bets that the market would decline substantially—and soon. It is not an exaggeration to say Marty was, indeed, betting that the stock market would crash. This is not to say that Marty was *hoping* for a tragic event to occur. But his intellectual curiosity brought him to this inevitable place where he believed the market's record rally would end tragically, just as it had before. Marty's mathematical calculations suggested that if the market were to decline, it would have to decline about 20% to correct the excesses generated over the last many months. He thought it possible that modern trading techniques would allow that to happen in a single day, thanks to the technological advances that sped up all the action in the financial markets.

Convinced that such an implosion was coming, Marty began the search for the option vehicle that would allow him to make maximum profits on the coming crash in stocks. He settled on put options on the Standard & Poor's

500 futures contract. Put options increase in value as the market goes down. So if the market declined big, as Marty guessed it would, the options would skyrocket and he would be rich. It was a double derivative play that utilized very cheap options contracts. The trade allowed Marty to load up on these arcane instruments at a very low cost. But if he was right, they would explode in value. If he was wrong, he would lose thousands of dollars.

The put options that Marty bought for his own account, for his mother, sister, clients, and for his firm, were unbelievably inexpensive. The puts were so cheap because they were "out of the money," as they say in the options business. In other words, the price of the option was so far below the price of the underlying market index that a real calamity would have to occur for the index to fall back to that level. Marty bought his put contracts at 1/16 of a dollar apiece. He bought thousands and thousands of contracts. He even lent his mother $5,000 to join in the trade.

The Dow Jones industrial average had peaked in August, climbing to a then-record of 2722 and change. But as interest rates subsequently rose in the United States, the dollar went into free fall. Trade tensions with Germany rose and President Reagan engaged Iran in the Persian Gulf. Suddenly the "permanent plateau of prosperity" in the stock market was looking quite temporary, indeed. By September the market was coming unglued. By October, the meltdown Marty envisioned had begun. Still, investors remained confident that the downdraft in the stock market would pass as September, the worst month of the year for stocks, wound to a close.

Marty Martino was not so sure. He saw the market's big decline as imminent. He sprang into action in early October, sensing that timing was of the essence. He bought up all the cheap put options he could find. Then, two weeks later, disaster struck.

In the week ending October 16, the Dow shed another 350 points. Marty's put options soared in value. From 1/16, they vaulted to $9 each, each contract worth 144 times what Marty paid for it. On October 16th alone, the Dow dropped over 100 points in a single day, the largest point decline in market history! Was this the crash Marty had feared would come? He nervously thought about taking profits on his trade.

For all intents and purposes, the market *had* essentially crashed in September and October. The Dow had gone from 2722 in August to 2240 on October 16, a stunning 480 point decline in less than two months. But Marty waited another day to sell, sensing that the crescendo to this market arpeggio was still at hand.

By now, everyone knows the story of Black Monday. October 19, 1987, was the worst day in stock market history. The Dow Jones industrial average cratered 508 points, or 22.5% in a single day! The value of Marty's put options exploded from 1/16 of a dollar apiece to an unbelievable $50 dollars each—800 times their original price! Marty's mother saw her $5,000 investment turn into $4 million. Marty's firm, his clients, his sister and, of course, he made a killing from the market's descent. He had done his homework and had been rewarded for achieving a level of understanding few others had come close to duplicating. He was both good and lucky, it seemed.

But the devastation the crash wreaked on Wall Street led Marty to believe that he'd never get paid for his insights. If Wall Street collapsed, even profitable transactions might not pan out. Options trading is a zero-sum game. For every winner, there is a loser. Marty bought his put options from other traders. They lost all the money he made! If they were out of business, who would pay him his due?

Lucky for Marty, though, the system didn't fail. Wall Street downsized as a result of the crash, but the system survived and Marty got his money. Had the system not survived, Marty surmised later, it really wouldn't have mattered. Everyone would have been in the same boat—to the soup kitchen. Marty's trades ultimately cleared. He made "millions and millions and millions of dollars." He refused to say exactly how much he made, but others have verified his story. He made millions. Wall Street lore says he made $13 million.

Marty walked away from Wall Street in 1989 and moved to a lavish ski resort community in the Midwest, where he's watching his children grow up day by day. He still trades in and out of markets. He's even planning another big bet. He thinks the precious metals, particularly gold, are as dangerously undervalued today as stocks were overvalued in 1987.

Once again he is in the minority. But knowing what you know now, would you bet against Marty Martino?

Wang Lee

Wang Lee* was a "naked premium seller," as they say in the options business. That did not mean that Wang stood on the floor of the Chicago Board Options Exchange

---

*This is a fictitious name for a real person.

(CBOE) wearing nothing but a smile, selling options to any and all takers. No. In options parlance, it meant that Wang Lee was a trader who made his living selling options, but never hedging any of his trading activities. He was "naked" because on every transaction, Wang was vulnerable to big moves in the market, both up and down. His nakedness would one day leave him with nothing but the clothes on his back. Such is the nature of a trader's life.

Wang Lee was a Hong Kong investor who had a seat at the CBOE. He had become a huge player in the options market in the years leading up to the 1987 crash, amassing a cash horde of $12 million by Wednesday, October 14, 1987. Being a naked premium seller was the most speculative and dangerous job in the trading pits.

Wang of Hong Kong sold options that were priced well above or well below the price of a stock market index, known as the Standard & Poor's 100, for a living. (The S&P 100 is known on the floor of the CBOE as the OEX, options exchange index.) He used to sell "out of the money" puts and calls on this benchmark index. For those sales, he received payments from the options buyers. Wang earned the "premium," as it's called, while the options buyers waited to see if their bets in the options market paid off.

If the market rallied or fell sharply, the options buyers made money. If the market failed to reach any of the prices on the options Wang sold, he would make money, since options that did not achieve their target prices by expiration expired worthless. Wang got to pocket the premium he was paid for selling the options in the first place. The farther away from the market the options were priced, the less likely it was that they would ever be "in the money." So, needless to say, Wang Lee sold options that were way "out of the money." Also needless to say, Wang made a lot of money doing it.

Professional options traders like Wang generally sell options to the buying public. But when they do, they usually take offsetting positions in the underlying securities to limit their risk. For example, if they sell an OEX call to an option buyer, they, by the virtue of their sale, have "shorted the market." Selling a call option is essentially a bet that stock prices will go down, since they are selling away the right to buy the underling stock. If the market goes up, the buyer makes money and the seller loses money.

To hedge that exposure, a call option seller might buy the actual, underlying stock index as a hedge. In this way, if the OEX goes up, the call option may decline in value, but the stock index will rise in price, offsetting the option seller's losses. Opposite strategies are employed when the option seller sells a put.

Now, if this is not complicated enough, there are traders like Wang Lee, the naked premium seller. Wang sold both puts and calls on the OEX, without ever hedging his exposure to big market moves. He sold options, pure and simple and never, ever covered his trader's ass.

As long as the market remained range-bound, or as long as it climbed slowly and steadily, Wang would make money on his options sales. If the market exploded to the upside, or imploded on the downside, then the options he sold would become valuable to the buyer, meaning that Wang Lee would owe the buyers money for making the correct bet. Naked premium selling is almost like being a bookie. It's a great business 'til somebody beats the spread.

Wang made great book for much of 1986 and 1987, when the stock market rallied predictably and steadily. By

October 14, 1987, his options sales had earned an incredible capital base for an individual trader working alone. But only five short days later Wang Lee would forever disappear from the trading floor.

On October 19, the Dow plunged 22%. Other market averages, like the OEX, plummeted a similar amount. That meant that all the put options Wang Lee had, presumably, sold safely were suddenly worth money to the buyers. And that meant, of course, that the put options were huge liabilities to Wang Lee. The decline was so great that Wang's profit of $12 million dollars turned into losses of $75 million—almost overnight. He was wiped out.

If Wang had been a bookie, it would have been as if a rookie basketball player on the underdog team threw up a Hail Mary shot at the buzzer, defeating the heavy favorite. The bookie would have had to pay everyone who bet the long shot at incredibly high odds. It was a career breaker.

Wang's fortunes took a $90 million turn in less than three days. He was finished. In fact he could not make good on all the options he sold. He simply didn't have the money to cover the losses. The pay off would be up to his clearing house, the firm that backed all of his trades.

As the story goes, First Options, a unit of Continental Bank, was forced to pony up the difference. In the week of the 1987 crash, Chicago was rife with rumors that First Options was about to go bankrupt, suffering under the weight of huge liabilities in the options market. The firm was saved only after its parent, Continental Bank, bailed it out. Ironically, Continental, itself, had been bailed out of insolvency by the Federal government only three short years before.

Singlehandedly, Wang Lee nearly broke the bank. His naked premium selling left an entire firm exposed to the cold that gripped the markets in the third week of October, 1987.

He has not been heard from since.

Few Options

Carl Sandburg dubbed Chicago "the city of big shoulders." In Chicago's futures pits, the inhabitants stand big shoulder to big shoulder, pushing and shoving in an effort to muscle their way to greater and greater profits on the trading floors. Whether it's the ancient Board of Trade, the Mercantile Exchange, or the relative newcomer to LaSalle Street, the Chicago Board Options Exchange, there is a raw energy on the floor that represents the primitive core of capitalism. On the trading floor, men and women shout, gesture, push, and shove their way toward bidding on a bit of the American dream. At times, the pits can look most unseemly, as individuals are crushed into a monetary mob, collectively engaged in an orgy of buying and selling in order to get and spend.

Few of Chicago's trading offers as clear a vision of that reality as the main trading pit at the Chicago Board Options Exchange. At the CBOE, there is a large pit that holds about four hundred traders. It is known as the OEX pit. It is there that options on a major stock market average, the S&P 100, are traded. The OEX options allow big institutions to hedge their positions in the stock market by buying or selling index options through the OEX pit. The OEX index is a basket of one hundred large company stocks that are frequently found in big investors' portfolios. As a result of the OEX's popularity, the OEX pit is a busy place where thousands of options contracts are bought and sold every day by the four hundred pit traders who walk the options floor.

Back in 1987, and for a few years before as well, the OEX options contracts were used as a key ingredient of some very complicated stock and options strategies that large institutions employed to either hedge their bets in the stock market, or to simply speculate in the wild bull market that had been roaring for several years in a row.

That bull market, as everyone now knows, came to a crashing end. But in the days and weeks before there were some wild happenings in the pits of the Chicago Board Options exchange.

In the week before the crash, the OEX pit was generally filled to its four-hundred-person capacity every day. In fact, there were days in which a thousand traders tried to cram into the space designed for less than half that number, as they grappled with a market that had seemingly gone berserk. Not only did scores of extra traders try to make their way into the pit, but once they got there they didn't want to leave. No trader worth his salt would walk away from such a chaotic market in which the opportunities to make money, and the risks of losing it, were so great.

Finding a good spot from which to trade was also of paramount importance. It was imperative one hold his spot in order to capture and keep the attention of the market-makers who executed their transactions at the center of the pit. Few traders left to take lunch breaks, or even bathroom breaks, for that matter, fearing the loss of one's position in the pit, or even worse, the loss of money from still another hiccough in the market.

Legend has it that one trader turned his own physical impairment into an advantage in the pit that year. This trader had suffered from a battle with colon cancer. He had survived the dread disease, but it left him unable to rid himself of waste in the traditional way. Colon cancer survivors are frequently fitted with a colostomy bag, a receptacle that collects waste into a pouch one wears outside the abdomen.

It is said that this trader put his bag to good use. During the height of the market's craziness in that wild week in 1987, he reportedly never once left the trading pit to relieve himself. Because he never lost his position on the floor, he was able to work the crowd far more effectively than others who required bathroom breaks.

As one senior CBOE staffer recalls, it was not too long before other traders were calling their physicians in an effort to get outfitted with one of the bags, just in case things on the floor really hit the fan.

Closing Rituals

On the Friday before the stock market crash, both the stock and options markets were going wild. It was a day of intense price swings, a day in which the Dow Jones industrial average plunged 103 points, the apparent culmination to a dismal week that had already trimmed a couple hundred points from popularly watched stock market gauges.

On Friday, October 16, a senior Options Exchange executive was giving a tour of the trading floor to several Japanese government officials, including Japan's associate minister of finance. The group was quite impressed by the flow of action on the floor and the seeming ease in which traders executed their positions, even in the midst of such market madness.

At the close of trading, many of the players in the pits were exhausted by the intense action of that day and were quite fearful that the sickening slide in stock prices might have put them or their firms out of business. (At that time, they had no idea that the following Monday would be far more frightful.)

Regrettably for the exchange official giving the tour, a public relations disaster was in the making. At the final bell, the day's maddening action had finally taken its toll on even the most savvy, veteran traders. A fight broke out in the pits, as players quarreled over some disputed trades. The pushing and shoving captured the attention of the Japanese guests, who watched the scuffle with great curiosity. They quickly inquired about the commotion that had taken center stage on the trading floor.

The senior exchange official brilliantly offered an explanation the Japanese could appreciate.

"We have closing rituals," he said, moving them on to another area of the trading floor.

The Japanese delegation nodded and smiled, offering its seal of approval for this ritualistic display taking place in the pits.

"WE HAVE CLOSING RITUALS"

An Author's Tale

In October of 1987, I traveled to the Windy City for a small break from the rigors of reporting financial news. A long-time buddy of mine was in medical school at the time, training at Chicago's Northwestern University. As old buddies are wont to do, he invited me out to run amok on the streets of Chicago, promising that from Rush Street to Michigan Avenue, a good time would be had by all.

With an offer too good to turn down, I planned to take in the sights and sounds of the City of Big Shoulders, to soak up the second city's famous jazz, to visit its impressive Art Institute, and to consume humongous portions of Giordano's spinach-stuffed pizza. It is a trip I recommend wholeheartedly.

I had, at that time, also grown quite curious about the wild world of derivative vehicles that were becoming ever more popular in the investment community. Ironically, those derivatives, like stock options and stock index futures, found a home in Chicago. They were traded at Leo Melamed's Mercantile Exchange or Duke Chapman's Options Exchange. As I planned my trip to Chicago, I reserved some time to make a pilgrimage to the mecca of the derivatives world, found on the corner La Salle and Whacker. It is there that the three options and futures temples exist.

Ironically, the Options Exchange was offering an options trading class near the week I had planned to visit town. With a quick schedule alteration, I moved my departure date to October 17, 1987. I did not know it then, but this vacation would turn out to be the most valuable experience of my entire career.

The week before I left for Chicago was a wild one in the financial markets. Computerized program trading and portfolio insurance programs had caused intense gyrations in the stock market. The programs made great use of complex options and futures-related trading strategies, strategies I would come to know firsthand, in a matter of days. I left Los Angeles in the third week of October, headed for Carl Sandburg's mythical city.

As fate would have it, the following Monday morning, was *the* Monday morning, the day of the Crash. Needless to say, the options seminar I planned to attend was canceled almost immediately upon starting. Some twenty-five Paine-Webber brokers in attendance were sent back to their home offices to deal with panicky customers.

Crash Tales

As for me, I made the first of many live appearances on FNN reporting, quite accidentally, from the floor of one of the country's busiest and most upset marketplaces. I did no fewer than seven live reports on the day of the crash. It was one of the most valuable "vacations" I ever took. I worked the entire week, reporting frequently from the floor of the CBOE, explaining to a rather confused audience how the whacky world of derivatives had influenced the course of events in the financial markets that memorable week.

One of my most vivid memories, however, has little to do with the actual chaos and carnage that took place that week. What stands out in my mind most is just how long it took anyone in the markets to laugh about the tragedy.

I don't say this to be callous about the devastation that the crash wrought on some traders' lives. It was, however, notable that this group of quick-witted, fly-by-the-seat-of-your pants professionals failed to employ any of the gallows humor they normally spew out during tragic events.

Remember that in the moments immediately after the explosion of the space shuttle, *Challenger*, trading floors from New York to Chicago were brimming with shuttle jokes. So too after the McDonald's Massacre that took twenty lives in San Diego not long before. But in the moments, hours, and even days after the crash, levity was nowhere to be found.

Finally, on Thursday, October 22, one of the floor traders I had come to know approached me with a few crash jokes. Tom Brady, then the director of floor operations for Thompson McKinnon, cornered me in my perch in the gallery and peppered me with several of the now-famous market rib-ticklers.

"What do you call a yuppie broker?" he asked.

"Oh, Waiter. . . ."

Or, "How do you get a yuppie broker out of a tree?"

"Cut the rope."

Or, "What's the difference between a yuppie broker and a pigeon?"

"A pigeon can still make a deposit on a BMW."

After he was through, I posed a simple question.

"Hey Tommy, how come it took you four days to come up with any jokes? When the space shuttle crashed, the jokes were flying off the trading floor in seconds. But then, those people only died. You guys lost money!"

"Good point" was about all Tom had to say.

Street Talk

Wall Street has forever been a wild place, from its financial excesses to its more notorious behavioral excesses. But the Street is no longer the male bastion it once was. Given the changes in the workplace and society as a whole, the sophomoric pranks and the rampant skirt-chasing has toned down considerably. The old boys network, while still extant, is not quite the network it once was.

The Predators' Ball

Mike Metrenko, the oldest member of the New York Stock Exchange recalls his early days on the Street, in the 1920s and 1930s, when he'd take his compatriots from the floor back to Scranton, Pennsylvania. There, the local ladies of the evening waited. Many of his colleagues would head for the dingy little mining town late on a Thursday or Friday night, telling their wives there was business to do in "Buffalo" and they'd be back by late Saturday afternoon.

In later years, there would be similar tales of lustful behavior. Connie Bruck, author of *The Predators' Ball*, chronicled the exploits of Drexel Burnham Lambert and its clients at the Beverly Wilshire Hotel, where their clients and a handful of consorts would reportedly do business in the now-infamous Bungalow 8. Client service has always been an important aspect of doing business on Wall Street!

And it has ever been thus, although the Street today is much more tame than it once was. Maybe because women are more prominent on Wall Street now than they used to be, and the old boy network is fading into history. Or maybe the crush of business has simply become too heavy to allow much play time. In any event, the Street is not the animal house it used to be.

Back in the early 1970s, Willie Montana* was an up-and-coming star in the money management business. He was a bachelor, living the good life in Manhattan, after growing up in the quiet solitude of a slightly southern state. He was not, though, a big-time ladies man—as were many of his contemporaries in the early years of the "me decade."

Still he enjoyed the ladies. Willie recalls a phone call from a friend, many years back, inviting him to a party that would be dominated by brokers and traders. It would be a typical industry gathering where the group could relax and enjoy each other's company after a rough day in the trenches.

In addition to the usual collection of market regulars, Willie remembers being bowled over by the plethora of beautiful women populating the place. Money, as we know, is a most powerful aphrodisiac.

Willie managed to hit it off with one of the female attendees, a gorgeous young thing, who found him charming,

*Willie Montana is a fictitious name. The real Willie asked to remain anonymous.

witty, and urbane. He was quite taken with her as well. After a few hours, a few drinks, and a little small talk, Willie brags of how the young lady asked him to walk her home, fearing the mean streets of New York might be inhospitable at such a late hour. Always the gentleman, Willie obliged, walking her to her flat. He hoped he could convince her to see him again, maybe for dinner and drinks in the coming days.

The blonde bombshell invited him in for a drink, and before he knew it, Willie had been hailed the conquering hero.

Feeling quite manly, Willie strode into work the next morning, walking just a few inches taller than usual. His friend, who had invited him to the swank gathering, inquired as to whether or not he had a good time.

"Are you kidding," Willie asked. "The party was great."

"Well, did you get lucky?"

"Absolutely," Willie said proudly. "She was terrific."

Willie's pal burst his bubble in an instant.

"Did you know every woman at the party was a hooker? Each one, bought and paid for."

Willie has since become a ladies' man—one lady's man. He likes it better that way.

A Room with a View

The "morning call" is market slang for a companywide conference that financial firms use to communicate

Evening Corn Comment Wed Aug 1993
from Charlie Sernatinger

Buyers: Bache 1.2 mln sep, Contl 1.2 mln sep, PW 1.0 mln dec, Term 1.2 mln dec

Sellers: Cargill 1.3 mln dec, Gerald 1.0 mln dec, MLP 1.0 mln dec

Spreaders: Ref 1.8 mln sep-dec 1 3/4, RR 1.0 mln sep-dec 1 3/4, GSA 2.0 mln dec-sep 1 1/2

Options: Ref sold 400 dec 220 calls & puts, Contl bot 300 dec 210 puts

Summary: Two sided commercial trade, funds dumping long corn short wheat spreads.

NEWS

Once again the funds dumped long corn short wheat spreads, among other things, with the technicians now thinking we will test the $1.06 level again shortly in Dec. Demand is still good in the nearby with Zimbabwe buying most of their PL 480 tender (one cargo off the Atlantic), Morocco in the market and Taiwan back in next week along with various dibs and dabs of onesies and twosies. Weather looks warm for the weekend, but the cold front returns supposedly next Tuesday, so get your sticks out while you can. The 6–10 day was normal. Deliverable stocks fell again with Chicago down 500,000 at 2.9 mln and Toledo down 600,000 at 6.3 mln, so spreads are still coming in and the floor won't be

Street Talk

happy until the spread trades even money in the Sep-Dec. Again, no Carla Hills announcement as the administration tries the diplomatic road in high level negotiations before pissing everyone off by throwing tarifs on everything under the sun. Open interest was down 8.5 mln yesterday. For you technicians, the Elliot Wavers think today's break was the "B" break in a "4" wave correction—whatever that means. In plain English, they think we have seen the interim setback with a move in Dec back up to 230. Look lower to start, higher to close on short covering. *Off the grain floor, the Chicago Board of Trade had its own convention of sorts yesterday afternoon as literally hundreds of late afternoon inhabitants of offices in the glassed-in atrium annex of the CBT building left their offices and gathered to gape at an extraordinary exhibition. In a 17th floor glass office opening into the interior of the atrium, a nubile young (female) phone clerk from the Refco firm and a hitherto unnamed soybean option broker (with the initials "ACT" on his badge) were caught "in flagrante delicto" engaging in the act of love while back office workers from many of the CBT clearing firms cheered them on, the participants having apparently forgotten to lower the blinds on the windows. Perhaps most extraordinary, the young lady actually showed up for work on the floor this morning, although the broker declined to attend. This being the biggest talk on the floor seemed to me to deserve mention, since there is clearly nothing else to talk about today . . .*

Note: Italics added for emphasis.

Source: Charlie Sernatinger.

183

their trading and investment plans for each and every day. On the morning call, economists predict and analyze the latest economic numbers released by the government. Market strategists offer their opinions on the stock and bond markets. Traders discuss featured stocks and trading strategy, and so on, and so on. The morning call can be a relatively lively interchange, or it can be quite boring and uneventful. It all depends on what's going on in the world of business and finance.

There are some days in the financial markets when the action gets a little dull, a little lifeless, sometimes even painfully boring. But traders always find ways to break the monotony.

One such instance occurred a few years ago at the Chicago Board of Trade and was reported during morning call by Charlie Sernatinger.

Sernatinger is a grains analyst and broker for E. D. F. & Man, an international commodity firm that has offices all over the world. An irascible type, he makes his home in the company's Chicago offices, where he landed in the autumn of 1993. He was fired from Smith Barney, a fortnight prior, for publishing the following observation about "the morning after":

Charlie's description of The Act landed him in the unemployment lines. He had committed the ultimate sin. Since his morning comments were widely distributed to clients and fellow brokers, the widespread publicity embarrassed Smith Barney and the Chicago Board of Trade. The official line on Charlie's departure described it as a "voluntary" separation. Charlie Sernatinger says they fired him for his own prosaic proclivities.

The Bear

Wall Street has a long and storied history of being populated by prodigious drinkers. At least that's the way one Wall Street wag describes some of his memories about his days on the Street. A case in point was "The Bear." The Bear was a veteran of Wall Street's many wars. He was also among the most prodigious consumers of spirits in lower Manhattan. Traders and brokers are full of stories regaling their wild days when they frequented the street's colorful cabarets and saloons. Many evenings were spent sipping the scotch and bragging of the day's successful campaigns—and lamenting some of the street's bloodier financial battles.

As for The Bear, his story is told by another grizzled veteran of Wall Street, Art Cashin. As Cashin recalls The Bear's story, he was heading home one night after a grueling day in the market and an equally gruelling night at one of Wall Street's favorite watering holes. The Bear was "overtrained" from dipping his muzzle a little too deeply into the honey pot. Not that this was an unusual experience: The Bear, like many of his coworkers, got "ahead of the count" occasionally, but most of the time he managed to make it home from work and back again the next day. Not this time.

It was a rough road back to Little Silver, New Jersey, a Wall Street bedroom community on the Jersey shore, that like many New Jersey hamlets offered a welcome quiet from the hectic pace of lower Manhattan

The Bear traveled home by train at the end of every day, and it was a good thing, because on many days he was probably in no condition to operate heavy machinery.

"Where's the nexsht train to Little Shilver," he slurred.

"Already gone," came the response from the ticket clerk.

"When's the nexsht one out?"

"There the 10:07, sir."

"Does it have a bar car?"

"No, sir!"

"Which train *has* a bar car?"

"The one over there on Track b, but . . ."

"Thanks, buddy!"

The Bear began lumbering over to the tracks, like a groggy beast just coming out of a season-long hibernation.

"But sir, that train isn't going to New Jersey."

No response.

"Sir, that train's not going to Jersey," wailed the young clerk, sensing The Bear was in for a rather long and difficult journey.

"Don't care," said The Bear, as he boarded the Montrealer.

The next morning, The Bear called in from Canada.

"I don't think I'll make it into work today," he told his associates.

Gutter Ball

Bedroom conquests are a frequent feature of the tales told on Wall Street. Indeed traders tell, with great relish, stories about their personal exploits. And they tell about the exploits of others who, in some way, stood out from the crowd. All of the players on the Street want to be the stuff of legend. Some achieve that by their skill in the business and still others by outlandish behavior.

One tale stands out for its audacity and for its ability to illustrate how the quick-thinking mind of a trader can save him from even the most precarious plight.

This may be an apocryphal tale from the Street, since the storytellers refuse to name the trader in question. However, it's told by reliable sources. They tell this tale with great relish because it proves a trader with balls is the best trader of all.

Buddy* is a rather large and oafish character, something of a couch potato at home. But he's a killer on the job—a prized player and quite a successful stock trader. He is not an attractive man, but he does have money. His success has brought not only a wife and kids, but also a little chippie on the side.

Buddy's most daring exploit off the floor is to meet his girlfriend every Thursday night. He achieves this deceit in a most cunning way.

To ensure the regularity of his dangerous liaisons, Buddy concocted a story that anyone familiar with Wall Street would almost immediately doubt. He told his loving and guileless wife that the New York Stock Exchange started a bowling league which he was immediately planning to join. The reason anyone familiar with Wall Street might doubt the story is that Exchange members are not, usually, members of the bowling class. Their endeavors usually involve more urbane pursuits, like horseback riding for the active or bridge for the thoughtful.

---

*The name has been changed to protect the guilty.

Be that as it may, Buddy said the league scheduled its events every Thursday, so his presence would be required weekly. He was pleased to do his part, knocking down pins for the Big Board's new team. Buddy feigned excitement over the prospects of getting a little exercise to boot, some calorie burning of which he was in desperate need.

His wife was thrilled that this lump would finally be getting some activity instead of his enduring his nightly potato-chip lifting exercises. Jubilant that Buddy's life might be extended by this sudden interest in physical activity, Buddy's loving wife surprised him with a gift—a bowling ball presented to him on his birthday.

Buddy seemed quite pleased with his new toy. He graciously accepted the gift and promptly dropped it into the back seat of his car, never removing the sixteen-pound orb from its leather bag, not even to look at it.

Henceforth, each Thursday night, Buddy would stay in the city, telling his wife there was no point driving home after a grueling night at the lanes, when he'd just have to drive back to Manhattan early the next day. His wife, accustomed to the notion that many traders spent weeknights in the city, accepted his alibi without question. Friday evenings, Buddy would arrive at home, just plumb tuckered out from "bowling night" and from a final day of trading on Wall Street.

A few months later on a quiet Sunday afternoon, his wife suggested that she and Buddy take the kids to the local lanes for a little family outing. They could be together as a unit and Buddy would be able to demonstrate his newly found athletic abilities to the kids. It would be fun, she told him.

Street Talk

Buddy happily obliged. Shoes rented, balls handed out, the happy family got ready to play. Buddy, armed with his birthday ball, still neatly housed in its leather bag, pulled the orb from the pouch, only to find, to his horror, the ball had no holes.

Being a trader whose mind is conditioned to think quickly in all sorts of tricky situations, Buddy explained how he's been bowling with this ball for months. His fingers swelled every day from writing out an unending number of stock market tickets, he explained, so they couldn't fit in a bowling ball's holes. On a busy day traders are as much scribes as they are traders. His alibi solid, Buddy spent the rest of the day showing off his technique. He pushed the ball down the lane, two handed, from between his legs, a perfectly round and unholey ball careening endlessly into the gutter.

Constellations and Calendar Quirks

Traders in any marketplace can be a quirky bunch. Some are well grounded in market realities—trading only off concepts in which they are fully versed. Others trade superstitiously as we saw with Mitchell Mouse. Still others use calendar quirks, astrological events, or arcane and strange theories to guide their trading operations.

Few, if any, of those practices, can guarantee profits for the traders who employ them. But traders are always looking for an edge. One place they find that edge is in the repetitive behavior of the traders around them. The markets, which are nothing more than a reflection of the people in them, often behave the same way, at the same time of year, over and over and over again.

$igns of the Zodiac

Nearly every trader on Wall Street has a system for beating the market. Some traders verse themselves in the fundamental realities of a particular company's business.

Constellations and Calender Quirks

They review earnings reports, balance sheets, interest rates, and other aspects of business that could affect a company's stock price. Other traders rely on the use of charts that illustrates a stock's price movement over time. These technical analysts also use charts to predict the overall market's performance, using the past to predict the future. Still others use complex quantitative and statistical models for trading. Finally, the "rocket scientists" of Wall Street use rather arcane proprietary methods to help them trade: oscillators, speed lines, gann angles, spiral calendars, Elliott Waves, or other indicators of market behavior.

Then there is Arch Crawford. Arch Crawford is a market newsletter writer who makes his trades based on the position of the planets and other astronomical phenomena. A quirky calling to some. But to Arch, the correlation between the movements of the Sun, Moon, and stars and the financial markets is there for all to see, if one only knows where to look in the cosmos.

From his own description, Arch Crawford was a somewhat precocious child, always interested in numbers—extracting square roots for fun in his younger days. One day little Arch saw a page of numbers in the newspaper that piqued his curiosity. He was told they were stock prices and that they went either up or down from day to day. Most important, he was told that he could make money from the daily fluctuations in stock prices.

Arch asked incredulously, "You mean I can make money without working?" He was hooked. (He has since found out the art of investing does, indeed, take a lot of work.)

So, at the tender age of twelve, Arch Crawford began keeping track of stock prices. He became an avid student of the stock market, reading Bernard Baruch's *My Own Story*. He also read great tales of moneyed men, like *The Robber Barons* and *How I Made $2,000,000 in the Stock Market*.

Arch's mind raced with possibilities. He began watching his first stock faithfully every day. He charted the course of Allegheny Corporation, a lumbering amalgam of Depression-era railroads that had seen its share of troubles in recent years. Arch tracked the stock, watching it drop to $7, bounce to $10 or $11 and hold steady over time. It was building a base for a big breakout to the upside, Arch surmised, employing the jargon of a budding technician.

He made his first purchase of Allegheny at $11 a share. It promptly went to $4. As they say on Wall Street, if you like it at eleven, you'll love it at four. So, Arch doubled up on the stock at $4. After waiting a year for the stock to skyrocket, Arch had had enough. He sold out his entire position at $11. He only made a little money, but he was wedded to the market for life.

Some years later, after finishing high school and spending a little time in college, he dropped out of the University of North Carolina and went on to work for Merrill Lynch in Raleigh. There he furthered his appetite for stock market investing, marking a chalkboard with fresh stock prices as the ticker tape came through the office. He became an assistant bookkeeper and eventually made his way to Merrill's New York office. It was in New York where Arch really learned how to chart the market. He served as the first assistant to Robert Farrell, a Wall Street legend who was among the first chartists to bring a certain respectability and intelligence to the field of technical analysis. Along with men like Edson Gould, Joe Granville, and a few others, Farrell ranks among the most prominent chartists Wall Street ever produced.

While Crawford learned the ins and outs of technical analysis from the revered Farrell, his insatiable curiosity about a host of topics was piqued by an article that appeared in the *Wall Street Journal* back in 1963. Profiled in the article was one Lieutenant Commander David Williams, who had written an exhaustive study of the link between Wall Street and the cosmos. It was called *Financial Astrology*. Soon after reading that piece of work, Arch discovered a 1940s pamphlet entitled "Stock Market Prediction," written by Donald Bradley. The booklet ascribed values to the degrees of separation in planetary alignment. The values were related back to the behavior of the stock market.

By this time, Arch, too, had coincidentally developed more than a passing interest in astronomy and astrology. He owned books describing planetary positions dating back to 1890. As he became more familiar with the history of the market, he found that various planetary positions and alignments frequently coincided with certain types of market behavior. Nonthreatening harmonic angles coincided with stock market tops. Eclipses, and the squaring of planets, and other more threatening cosmological developments, often coincided with extreme volatility in stock prices. These discoveries led Arch to a market method that combined the strict practice of charting stocks with the less precise science of charting the stars.

Interestingly enough, today Arch only looks at the statistical correlation between certain cosmological phenomena and significant market events. In other words, he doesn't profess to know why certain extraterrestrial events lead to market euphoria or distress. He only knows that they are somehow linked. When Arch sees a positive astrological development on the horizon, so to speak, he will buy stocks. When more ominous celestial activity occurs, he exits the market.

While he doesn't profess to know why the stars influence the Street, he does note that the work of John H. Nelson comes closest to offering a causal relationship between the swirling of the heavens and the gyrations on Wall Street. Nelson's work attempts to show that by looking at the movements and alignments of the planets one can accurately predict sunspot activity. At this point, no doubt, your eyes are starting to glaze over. But, don't fall asleep yet.

Some cosmological theorists have speculated that sunspot activity alters human behavior on Earth, causing bouts

TRIPLE WITCHING FRIDAY

of mass euphoria or anxiety. Some believe that happens because sunspot activity disrupts the normal electricity in the Earth's magnetic field. And that disruption of the ionosphere just might lead to bouts of collective euphoria or despair, two phenomena which often visit themselves upon financial markets.

In any event, it seems that for some time, Arch's cosmological leanings have left him on terra firma when it comes to the stock market. He is frequently among the most highly rated market newsletter writers on Wall Street. He has made some great calls on the market and he has also been wrong as frequently. But like the girl with the curl, when he's right, he's very, very right, as the next anecdote shows.

A Little Lunacy

In 1987, the "harmonic convergence" took Wall Street by storm. This harmonic convergence was a long-awaited celestial event that brought five of the solar system's nine planets into their tightest alignment in over 800 years. The stock market, coincidentally or not, hit an all time high on August 25, 1987, at 2722. It would be the highest level the market would reach before crashing by 1,000 points over the next two months. The market's vicious decline culminated in a 508 point drop on October 19, 1987. That was Black Monday, as it is now remembered on Wall Street. The harmonic convergence, a most welcome event, curiously struck when Wall Street was in the midst of a collective "high." The euphoria peaked as the convergence took place. As Mickey Rourke's character once said in the movie *Diner*, "It's Ripleys."

Arch Crawford recalls that on August 24, 1987, the Sun, the Moon, Mercury, Venus, and Mars were in "one-third harmonic triangle to Jupiter." They were locked in the tightest planetary conjunction in at least 800 years, maybe longer, Arch reckons. According to Crawford's star charts, these five bodies will line up within 5–10° of one another. That happens about every 396 years. But in 1987, the five orbs were within 2 1/4° of one another, an unusually tight conjunction. It was an event that people the world over gathered to herald. There were communal rituals from California to Calcutta, as terrestrial beings communed with the cosmos. It was a period marked by a collective feeling of enlightenment and happiness.

The convergence also marked a peak in the euphoric mood on Wall Street. Armed with both terrestrial and extraterrestrial trading tools, Arch knew that the harmonic convergence represented a top in the stock market. On August 10, 1987, Arch penned a prediction for a publication known as *The O-T-C Journal*, a stock market letter in which he outlined his bearish bent, recommending that investors exit the stock market ahead of an imminent crash. He told investors to buy Treasury bills, gold, and stock index put options, options that would rise in value if the stock market fell. He called for the market to top with the advent of the harmonic convergence and crash shortly thereafter. It did. On October 19th, the stock market suffered its worst day in the history of stock market trading.

It was easy to see it coming. All one had to do was look up at the sky.

Quirks of the Calendar

That traders like a sure thing is a given on Wall Street. There's nothing like knowing, with absolute certainty, that one is going to make money without any risk. So to that end, market participants and observers study the patterns the market follows. Since the dawn of time all kinds of history tends to repeat. Traders look at the calendar to determine whether stock prices behave a certain way at any given time of year. And lo and behold they do. And the trading patterns give rise to old adages on Wall Street, truisms that suggest the market has, and always will behave a particular way on a particular day. "Sell Rosh Hashanah, buy Yom Kippur" is one saying that describes how the market sells off in September and tends to bottom out in the month most everyone on Wall Street has learned to fear— October. Traders also talk of a "summer rally." There's also the "Santa Claus rally," the "January Barometer," the "January Effect," the "Presidential cycle," just to name a few periods in which the market is expected to do what it, seemingly, always does.

Yale Hirsch, who publishes *The Stock Trader's Almanac* was among the first observers of the stock market to make a career out of cataloguing the market's various calendar quirks. The New Jersey-based market historian has pored over the market's trading patterns for a lifetime, exploring and documenting the repetitive patterns and renewable cycles in stock market activity.

It was Yale who discovered the so-called Presidential cycle. Simply stated, the stock market generally encounters rough waters in the second full year of a new president's term. It is not always true, but it is quite frequently a reliable phenomenon. And the reason is quite simple. Most presidents want to be reelected, so to achieve that goal they are often advised to make their unpopular economic choices early in their terms. In most cases, new presidents will raise taxes, cut spending, accept higher interest rates from the Federal Reserve, even endure a recession early on if it means they can cut taxes, boost spending, or watch interest rates fall just as the election draws near. By gulping the bitter pills early, presidents are free to make those popular and economically stimulating decisions later on.

Hirsch's examination of market history found the second year of a new president's term to be the worst one. But he also found out that years ending in 5 that also represent midterm years for a president have historically been excellent years for stock market investing. Even better is a year ending in 5, that also includes the election of a new Congress. (By the way, 1995 was such a year.)

To prove the point, take recent history as an example.

In 1994, the second year of President Clinton's new term, the broad list of stocks got pummeled as the new president had completed his year-earlier program to raise taxes and cut government spending, all in an effort to rein in the federal budget deficit. Additionally, there were lingering concerns about the president's politically unpopular health-care reform efforts, efforts that devastated health care and medical stocks well into 1994. Overall, the average stock was down about 30% from its peak at some point in the year, meeting the classic definition of a bear market. Even the stalwart Dow Jones industrial average declined almost 10% at its worst point of the year. (It did manage, however, to pretty much break even by year's end.)

For Your Information:

On a short-term basis, after Republicans win, the market usually has a brief celebration rally followed by an often sharp, short-term selloff. After Democrats win, the market usually initially sells off and then recovers sharply. The table below tries to look at a longer-term picture, giving you the facts. The row for Democrat President and Republican Congress should probably be discarded, however, due to a lack of observations. My own bias would be to look at the fourth row down—i.e., Republican Congress with slow growth, low inflation, and nowhere stock prices.

—Ned

Gains for Stocks, Economy, and Inflation By Party of President and Majority Party in Congress 03/04/01–11/08/94

| | Percentage Gain per Annum | | | |
	Stocks (DJIA)	Indus. Prod.	Inflat. (CPI)	Time (Years)
Dem. President	5.7	5.6	4.9	41.7
Rep. President	4.0	2.2	1.7	52.0
Dem. Congress	6.5	4.9	4.4	65.7
Rep. Congress	0.8	0.9	0.3	28.0
Dem. Pres., Dem. Cong.	6.6	6.6	4.5	37.8
Dem. Pres., Rep. Cong.	−2.1	−3.7	8.7	4.0
Rep. Pres., Rep. Cong.	1.3	1.7	−1.1	24.0
Rep. Pres., Dem. Cong.	6.3	2.7	4.2	28.9
Total Period	**4.7**	**3.7**	**3.1**	**93.7**

Note: Party in control of Congress is determined by averaging percentage control in the Senate and percentage control in the House. Dates used in study are presidential inauguration dates.

Source: Ned Davis Research.

In 1995, just the opposite was true. Stocks exploded higher early in the year and were well into record territory at the time this book was being written. By the end of June, the Dow Jones industrials were up nearly 19%, a stellar gain in only six months time, again confirming the repetitive behavior of market cycles.

Incidentally, Ned Davis, a savvy student of the stock market, compiled a very interesting schematic on how the stock market fares under various combinations of political parties in the executive and legislative branches of government (see boxed copy on the previous page). Interestingly enough, the worst combination for stocks included a Democratic president and a Republican-controlled Congress, the combination the country has today. The picture on this indicator is mixed, with the market doing well in 1995 in the midst of a Republican-controlled Congress and a Democratic administration.

What no one has figured out yet is how the markets will fare with a third-party candidate in the White House and either of the two other parties in control of Congress. It's a new combination Wall Street may soon have to trade on.

Holy Holidays

Holidays are joyous times on Main Street. So too on Wall Street. The market gets revved up around holiday time, and it's almost no surprise that the good cheer that comes from days of celebration, inebriation, or just plain rest helps put stock traders in euphoric moods every so often.

Constellations and Calender Quirks

And so, the days before holidays are quite happy occasions on Wall Street.

One of Wall Street's happy trackers is John McGinley, a technical market analyst who also watches the quirks of the calendar. His mentor, Arthur Merrill, discovered many of the holiday trading patterns in the stock market, but John is now the keeper of the flame. Yale Hirsch is another flame-keeper who watches the behavior of stocks around holiday time. He, too, notes that stock prices have a tendency to rally on the days immediately preceding holidays.

To show why that is an important little calendar quirk to be aware of, consider the following: On any given day throughout the calendar year, stock prices are up 52% of the time. But on the days before major holidays, stock prices are up 68% of the time, a statistically meaningful deviation from the norm. On some days before market holidays, it's darn near impossible not to make money, if one is familiar with a little market history.

Take, for example, the day before Labor Day. Stock prices are up 79% of the time on this day, going back to the turn of the century. The day before the July 4th holiday is almost equally enticing as stock prices have risen 72% of the time, dating back to the early 1900s.

Now one might expect stock prices to fall before long weekends, since very few traders would be inclined to leave their market positions unattended for an extended period. But that is not the case. On nearly every day before a holiday, stock prices have a greater tendency to go up than to go down.

Let's switch calendars for a moment, to find quirks in other monthly measurements of the market. If one uses the Hebrew calendar, one will find that the period surrounding Rosh Hashanah and Yom Kippur are unusually volatile. In fact, there is an old admonition on Wall Street to "sell Rosh Hashanah and buy Yom Kippur."

The Jewish New Year usually comes in the Gregorian month of September. It just so happens that September is the worst month of the year for stock prices, according to Yale Hirsch's *Almanac*. Yom Kippur usually occurs in October, the month of the year that is most feared for its frequent massacres of stock market portfolios. But, in October, when stock prices seem to inexplicably plunge with great regularity, stocks also tend to bottom out. That's why one would "sell Rosh Hashanah and buy Yom Kippur!"

Now, back to the Gregorian calendar for a year-end wrap up. Historically, the last three months of the year have afforded stock market investors the greatest buying opportunities of the entire year. If one buys after a decline in October, as John McGinley points out, one is amply rewarded by his investments. Over time, the October through January period has been an exceptionally strong one for stocks. Even on Wall Street, there can be grace after the fall.

But wait, that's not all! There's also the Santa Claus rally that comes to town, nearly every year. There is also a very strong statistical tendency for the market to rally as a visit from St. Nick draws near. In the last thirty-five years, stock prices have jumped in the two weeks preceding Christmas about thirty times, which is better than getting a lump of coal in your stocking!

As the year begins anew on January first, there are some other important calendar quirks to keep in mind. The first is the January Barometer, a market indicator that claims, "as January goes, so goes the rest of the year" for stock prices. A strong January usually leads to a strong year for stocks, at least it has in the majority of years this century that have enjoyed bull markets in the first month of the year.

Don't forget, also, to keep an eye on the January Effect. That is a phenomenon in which small stocks do better than large stocks from the second week in December to the second week in January.

If all these little calendar tricks don't help you make money in stocks, try throwing darts at the calendar to pick the days on which you should buy stocks. There's a group of academics who say a random walk through the market will provide better results than any other system available. Oh, and when you're done investing, take a vacation in May; it's the third worst month of the year for Wall Street.

The Super Bowl

Now that we've mastered the quirks of the calendar on Wall Street, let's take a look at the quirkiest stock market indicator of all, the Super Bowl Theory.

What on earth does the Super Bowl have to do with stock prices? Absolutely nothing is the right answer. However, the Super Bowl Theory has the best track record of any market indicator anywhere, for anytime in the modern market era.

Here's how the theory goes. If an original team of the old National Football League (NFL) wins the Lombardi Trophy in January, stock prices will be higher come the end of that year. But if a team from the original American Football League (AFL) should prevail, it's going to be a rather rough year for stocks.* The Super Bowl Theory has accurately predicted the direction of stock prices 86% of the time since the first Super Bowl was played in 1967.

In that year and again in 1968, Vince Lombardi's Green Bay Packers trounced their AFL rivals, the Kansas City Chiefs and Oakland Raiders, by wide margins, guaranteeing a banner year for stocks. Indeed prices were rising wildly on Wall Street in the go-go years of the late 1960s.

But as 1969 drew to a close, the upstart New York Jets, led by "Broadway Joe" Namath, defeated the awe-inspiring Baltimore Colts, led by living legend Johnny Unitas. Nineteen sixty-nine was the last year to see rising stock prices before a series of bear markets gripped the streets. Nineteen sixty-nine was also the last year, for the next few, that an original NFL team took the world title in American football. The indicator has rarely failed to work since then. There have been some exceptions to the rule, as the accompanying chart points out. But for sheer coincidence, you just can't beat it.

The Super Bowl Theory is quite illustrative of a phenomenon economists like to call "false cause fallacies." Those are events that are seemingly related, but have little or nothing to do with one another. It's also a graphic illustration of how economists make up million dollar phrases to explain simple events. It's a coincidence, for God's sake!

---

*Some original NFL teams are now found in the American Football Conference, or AFC, like the Pittsburgh Steelers or the Indianapolis Colts. If they win the Bowl, it counts as an NFL victory, at least for the purposes of the theory.

Constellations and Calender Quirks

Super Bowl Theory Market Indicator Record

Year	Winner	Score	Loser	Score	Market
1967	Green Bay	35	Kansas City	10	S&P up 20.1%
1968	Green Bay	33	Oakland	14	S&P up 7.7%
1969	NY Jets	16	Baltimore	7	S&P off 11.4%
1970*	Kansas City	23	Minnesota	7	S&P up 0.1%
1971	Baltimore	16	Dallas	13	S&P up 10.8%
1972	Dallas	14	Miami	3	S&P up 15.7%
1973	Miami	14	Washington	7	S&P off 17.4%
1974	Miami	24	Minnesota	7	S&P off 29.7%
1975	Pittsburgh	16	Minnesota	6	S&P up 31.5%
1976	Pittsburgh	21	Dallas	17	S&P up 19.2%
1977	Oakland	32	Minnesota	14	S&P off 11.5%
1978	Dallas	27	Denver	10	S&P up 1.1%
1979	Pittsburgh	35	Dallas	31	S&P up 12.3%
1980	Pittsburgh	31	Los Angeles	19	S&P up 25.8%
1981	Oakland	27	Philadelphia	10	S&P off 9.7%

1982	San Francisco	26	
	Cincinnati	21	S&P up 14.8%
1983	Washington	27	
	Miami	17	S&P up 17.3%
1984*	LA Raiders	38	
	Washington	9	S&P up 1.4%
1985	San Francisco	38	
	Miami	16	S&P up 26.3%
1986	Chicago	46	
	New England	10	S&P up 14.6%
1987	NY Giants	39	
	Denver	20	S&P up 2.0%
1988	Washington	42	
	Denver	10	S&P up 12.40%
1989	San Francisco	20	
	Cincinnati	16	S&P up 27.25%
1990*	San Francisco	55	
	Denver	10	S&P off 6.56%
1991	NY Giants	20	
	Buffalo	19	S&P up 26.31%
1992	Washington	37	
	Buffalo	24	S&P up 4.46%
1993	Dallas	52	
	Buffalo	17	S&P up 7.06%
1994*	Dallas	30	
	Buffalo	13	S&P off 1.53%
1995	San Francisco	49	
	San Diego	26	S&P up 30.0%
1996	Dallas	27	
	Pittsburgh	17	S&P ?

*Exceptions to the theory.

Source: Rip Slusser at S&P MarketScope.

Constellations and Calender Quirks

One variation on the Super Bowl Theory. Arch Crawford, a stock market analyst who uses both technical analysis and astrology to chart the course of the market, uses the Super Bowl Theory in a unique way.

After analyzing the market through the use of technical analysis and astrological projections, Arch places his bets on the market. Then, he places a corresponding bet on the Super Bowl! If he sees the market going up, he'll bet on the original NFL charter member, no matter who it is. If he sees the market going down, he bets on the original AFL team. And who says playing the stock market isn't like gambling?

Name Index

Antolini, Bobby, 53–54
Aronstein, Michael, 124,
   127–131

Baron, Ron, 103–109, 138–144
Baruch, Bernard, 23, 147, 192
Benham, Jim, 110–112
Black, Prof., 161
Bliss, Frank E., 24–26
Bond, Ray, 23
Bradley, Donald, 193
Brady, Tom 177–178
Bramwell, Elizabeth, 66
Bruck, Connie, 179
Buffett, Warren, 56

Carr, Freddie, 63
Carter, Jimmy, 41
Cashin, Art, 6, 93, 185
Chapman, Duke, 176
Cochran, Tom, 93
Cohen, Abby Joseph, 66,
   78–81
Cohen, Paul, 108
Coleman, John C., 11–12
Cooperman, Leon, 135–138
Crawford, Arch, 191–195,
   196, 207

Dalton, Liam, 114–116
Davis, Ned, 199, 200

Dels, Don, 136
Dillon, Eastman, 25
Donaldson, William, 53
Donner, Fred, 98
Duer, William, 2–4

Einhorn, Steven, 78
Eisen, Harvey, 63

Farrell, Robert, 192
Finkel, David, 69
Fisher, Irving, 163
Ford, Gerald, 41, 137
Ford, Henry, 97

Garzarelli, Elaine, 66, 78
Gould, Edson, 192
Granville, Joe, 107, 192
Greenspan, Alan, 137
Gross, Bill, 55–57
Guttfreund, John, 56

Hamilton, Alexander, 2
Hanson, Chrissy, 23
Hirsch, Yale, 197–198, 201,
   202
Hulbert, Mark, 84–86

Iacocca, Lee, 97

Johnson, Ned, 118
Jones, Cathy, 73–78

Name Index

Kemp, Gil, 160
Kennedy, Ted, 54
Kerkorian, Kirk, 97, 100

Larkin, Jane, 71
Leeb, Steven, 84–86
Livermore, Jesse, 23
Lynch, Peter, 116–121

McCaw, Craig, 138
McGinley, John, 201, 202
Melamed, Leo, 40–48, 176
Merrill, Arthur, 201
Merriweather, John, 56
Metrenko, Michael, 22–27, 179
Milken, Michael, 3
Minter, Charlie, 128
Morgan, J. P., 23
Mozer, Paul, 56–57

Nelson, John H., 194
Nixon, Richard, 41

Oakley, Larry, 23

Pederson, Laura, 12–13
Pintard, John, 3

Raskob, John J., 22
Robertson, Julian, 159
Roffman, Marvin, 99–102, 103
Rogers, Jimmy, 145–154

Salvigsen, Stan, 128
Sandberg, Carl, 171
Sass, Martin, 131–134
Scavone, Bob, 11, 156–158
Scholes, Prof., 161
Scott, Edgar, 105–106
Seiden, Steve, 108
Sernatinger, Charlie, 182–184
Sheen, Charlie, 115–116
Siebert, Muriel, 65–72, 78
Smith, Al, 11, 20–21
Smith, Morris, 121
Soros, George, 146, 159
Spendly, Joe, 50–53
Sperandeo, Vic, 7, 17–18
Steinhardt, Michael, 159
Stern, Leonard, 140–141

Tabell, Tony, 103, 104
Towbin, Bob, 53–54
Trump, Donald, 99–102
Tsai, Jerry, 63, 70, 71

Unterberg, Tommy, 53

Vinik, Jeffrey, 118, 121–127

Yamani, Ahmed Zakj, 125
Young, John, 98

Williams, David, 193
Wynn, Steve, 99